Reconciling Mission

Reconciling Mission

Realizing God's Reign through Community Engagement

Alastair McKay and David Brubaker

Forewords by Samuel Wells and Nancy Ammerman

AN ALBAN BOOK

t&tclark
NEW YORK · LONDON · OXFORD · NEW DELHI · SYDNEY

T&T CLARK

Bloomsbury Publishing Inc, 1359 Broadway, New York, NY 10018, USA
Bloomsbury Publishing Plc, 50 Bedford Square, London, WC1B 3DP, UK
Bloomsbury Publishing Ireland, 29 Earlsfort Terrace, Dublin 2, D02 AY28, Ireland

BLOOMSBURY, T&T CLARK and the T&T Clark logo are trademarks of Bloomsbury Publishing Plc

First published in the United States of America 2026

Copyright © Bloomsbury Publishing Inc, 2026

For legal purposes the Acknowledgements on pp. xi–xii constitute an extension of this copyright page.

Cover design by Jen Huppert Design
Cover image © iStock.com/Zoran Zeremski., © iStock.com/CHUNYIP WONG

All rights reserved. No part of this publication may be: i) reproduced or transmitted in any form, electronic or mechanical, including photocopying, recording or by means of any information storage or retrieval system without prior permission in writing from the publishers; or ii) used or reproduced in any way for the training, development or operation of artificial intelligence (AI) technologies, including generative AI technologies. The rights holders expressly reserve this publication from the text and data mining exception as per Article 4(3) of the Digital Single Market Directive (EU) 2019/790.

Bloomsbury Publishing Inc does not have any control over, or responsibility for, any third-party websites referred to or in this book. All internet addresses given in this book were correct at the time of going to press. The authors and publisher regret any inconvenience caused if addresses have changed or sites have ceased to exist, but can accept no responsibility for any such changes.

Library of Congress Cataloging-in-Publication Data
available at http://lccn.loc.gov/2015040044

ISBN:	HB:	978-1-5381-9050-0
	PB:	978-1-5381-9051-7
	ePDF:	979-8-7651-6104-3
	eBook:	978-1-5381-9052-4

Typeset by Integra Software Services Pvt. Ltd.
Printed and bound in the United States of America.

For product safety related questions contact productsafety@bloomsbury.com.

To find out more about our authors and books visit www.bloomsbury.com and sign up for our newsletters.

Contents

List of Illustrations vi
Foreword: Samuel Wells, UK vii
Foreword: Nancy Ammerman, US ix
Acknowledgements xi

Introduction 1

1 Big Picture and Foundational Stories 13

2 Applying *Reconciling Mission* Insights in England 47

3 Collaborating to Meet Community Needs in Arizona 71

4 Raising Awareness and Pursuing Justice in Wisconsin 87

5 Neighborhood-Based Community Development in Montana 99

6 Applying an Asset-Based Approach in England 113

7 Concluding Threads 137

Notes 148
Recommended Further Reading and Resources 159
Index 164

List of Illustrations

1.1 Meeting Basic Human Needs 14
1.2 Raising Awareness of Injustice 17
1.3 Challenging the System 19
1.4 Transforming Systems 22
1.5 Realizing More of God's Reign 24
1.6 Theoretical Framework 25
1.7 Being Raised in Pharaoh's House 27
1.8 Killing an Egyptian 28
1.9 Learning in Midian 29
1.10 Confronting Pharaoh 30
1.11 Crossing the Red Sea 32
1.12 Journeying towards the Promised Land 33
1.13 Moses's Journey with Israel 34
1.14 Jesus's Infancy 35
1.15 Flight to Egypt 36
1.16 Learning in Nazareth 37
1.17 Driven into the Wilderness 38
1.18 Public Ministry: Confrontation 39
1.19 Crucifixion and Death 40
1.20 Resurrection 42
1.21 Jesus's Journey with Israel 43

Foreword UK

One of the first lessons I learned in community ministry was "Go where the energy is." I was blessed to spend my early years in ministry in the northeast of England, and was overwhelmed by the surplus energy in the community. A lot of this was because there was more talent than people were able to express through their often-mundane jobs—so much of ministry was finding constructive outlets for it.

Subsequently I served in parts of the country that didn't appear to have the same energy. But by then I'd learned the lesson and realized that the secret was not "Go where the positive energy is" but "Go where the energy is." Sometimes that energy could be dissipated in bitterness or grief or bottled up in depression. Nonetheless I'd learned that you can manufacture almost anything—except energy. Trying to drag a train up a hill is miserable: if gravity takes the train downhill, use the energy that's available.

This is a book about gauging, harnessing, refining, and amplifying energy. For many people today issues of justice stir the energy that once was put into community organizations and congregational life. The secret is to go where the energy is and work out how to unlock it. This is a book describing countless ways to do so.

The big reveal lying beneath the surface of the book is this: the theological term for energy is the Holy Spirit. Some people downplay community ministry because they suspect it doesn't "name the name" and keeps Jesus hidden. They forget Christianity is a trinitarian faith. The role of the Holy Spirit is to make Jesus present between the hour of his departure at the Ascension and the hour of his return. I have a description of the Holy Spirit: the Holy Spirit is Jesus out of control. The church doesn't get to dictate or decide where the Holy Spirit is at work making Jesus present.

Which is why community ministry is about going to find where the Holy Spirit is at work and joining in. This book, which celebrates community engagement, is actually something more far-reaching and more subversive: it's a theology of the Holy Spirit. Don't tell anyone: they won't like it; they may be celebrating having just got Jesus under control.

Revd Dr Samuel Wells,
Vicar of St Martin-in-the-Fields,
London, UK

Foreword US

A generation ago, the eminent sociologist Peter Berger approached me with a research idea – how exactly does religion relate to social change? When is it a cause? When is it transformed by other changes? He was given to such big questions. My counter to him was the proposal that it might be interesting to look at that question on a very local level. What happens when the immediate social world of the neighborhood changes? What do the congregations in those places do? After a couple of years on the ground in nine communities around the US, the book *Congregation and Community* attempted to answer that question.

But it also raised questions that have only gotten more pressing in the years since. How does one even define a "community," especially when the internet replaces physical presence with virtual? When people so freely choose commitments based on factors that have little to do with geographic place, does a church's neighborhood even matter? And when commitment to a congregation is limited or plural or nonexistent, how can that commitment extend to the church's neighborhood? Indeed, in a world of declining membership, how do congregations muster the wherewithal for any sort of engagement?

But people do still gather in real places. Those real places are the world to which many of them feel called to engage. This book gathers evidence from congregations that have done just that. They have done the hard work of defining what community means for them. They have figured out where they belong and claimed it, even if the boundaries don't quite fit any official municipal or ecclesiastical map. And they have gotten to know that place, patiently listening and intentionally providing opportunities for connection. Out of that listening, they have learned about both the strengths and the vulnerabilities around them. They have identified both the things that can easily be fixed and the things that are going to take time and perhaps more fundamental changes than they can manage.

By presenting us with cases from both the UK and the US, this book also makes clear that listening to each congregation's particular location matters. Polity and politics, economy and geography, history and recent transformations – all of it matters.

Across these cases, we also see congregations willing to reach out to find partners. They recognize that they cannot undertake their work alone. My later research (published in *Pillars of Faith*) asked about how congregations do their work, and the overwhelming answer for the work of community engagement was that they do it with partners. Not only do they need to pool resources, but what *Reconciling Mission* now adds is that congregations need to be working collaboratively because the listening does not stop when the issues are identified. It continues as people work together. Engagement is not a one-way street.

Perhaps once upon a time churches were indeed parishes, and their relationship to their communities was seamless. Not so today. Being engaged with a congregation's immediate neighborhood is not the mission to which every church is called. It is hard work and requires commitment, resources, and patience. Each church's theology will shape whether and how they engage. For those that are called to this path, the cases in this book will provide valuable wisdom.

Dr Nancy T. Ammerman,
Professor of Sociology of Religion, Emerita,
Boston University, USA

Acknowledgements

I, Alastair, am profoundly grateful to the many people who have contributed to or supported the writing of this book:

My wife, Sue, who stood by me through the long journey, and who kindly contributed the line drawings for Chapter 1.

The trustees of Reconciliation Initiatives, who have supported me throughout the organization's development and who released me to work on the manuscript for this book. This included kindly granting me a sabbatical in the autumn of 2023 to make a start on the book. Also Becky Gaskin, the administrator of Reconciliation Initiatives, who has provided gracious support and encouragement throughout.

All those whom I interviewed for the case studies in Chapter 2, not all of which I was able to draw on: Graham Adamson, Vicki Adamson and Mary Sapsford; Richard Westwood and Esther Allen; Luci Morriss and Ange Grunsell; Andrew Wickens and Paul Adams; and Phill Brown. As well as those who were interviewed for the Hodge Hill case study in Chapter 6: Al Barrett, Paul Wright, Penny Hall and Jane Perry. I greatly appreciated the openness and honesty of all my interviewees which has made this book so much the richer.

All those who have participated in the *Reconciling Mission* program who have lived out much of what is described in the book, and who have offered such encouragement to me and my colleagues in Reconciliation Initiatives over the last five years. Their helpful feedback has enabled the program to grow and evolve over that time.

My co-author, David Brubaker, who has given useful and honest feedback throughout the writing process and who has been such a blessing to collaborate with: I continue to appreciate his graciousness, patience and friendship.

I, David, am deeply grateful to my spouse, Mert, who supported my three research trips – to Arizona, Wisconsin, and Montana – as well as the time needed to transcribe and code interviews and develop draft chapters.

My own interest in congregations engaging their communities resulted from being a member of three engaged congregations in different US states. I am grateful for this lived experience with the Lancaster (Pennsylvania) Brethren in Christ Church, First Presbyterian Church of Casa Grande (Arizona), and Park View Mennonite Church (Virginia). Serving as a lay leader in each of these congregations taught me that community engagement can be demanding but also deeply rewarding.

I am also very appreciative of all those who participated in the interviews I conducted for this book, and particularly of the community members who coordinated my visits to each of the three communities where I interviewed religious and community leaders. These were Cindy Schaider in Casa Grande, Arizona; Marilyn Miller in Milwaukee, Wisconsin; and Kaleb Perdew in Billings, Montana.

Working with Alastair McKay has been one of the joys of my professional life, beginning with co-training together when Alastair was serving as director of Bridge Builders. As we continued to consult with congregations and their leaders over decades, we noticed that those congregations that engaged their neighborhoods and communities tended to be more resilient in times of conflict than those that remained isolated from their communities. This book grew out of that collaboration and insight.

Finally, we are both really grateful to Richard Brown and Victoria Shi, and their colleagues at Bloomsbury Publishing, for their support and encouragement throughout the publication process, enabling this book to arrive in your hands.

Introduction

Why This Book?

"Many religious congregations in North America and Western Europe are in terminal decline; they appear to have no future other than death." This is the prevailing narrative, told in various ways by sociologists, statisticians, and some religious leaders.

We—Alastair and David—are convinced that God is not finished with the church in our contexts. At the same time, we know that the church cannot continue with business-as-usual. If we are to see local congregations not just survive but thrive, something must change. Planting of new congregations, which often replicate the methods, approaches, and culture of their mother churches, is not sufficient. We believe that a deeper renewal is needed, where congregations across a broad theological spectrum partner with the Holy Spirit to engage in new ways with their neighbors and local communities.

God is always patiently at work, often in ways that faith communities have not noticed before. As members and leaders of local congregations, we need to open our eyes afresh, listen in new ways, and accept God's invitation to join in, in partnership with the Holy Spirit and our neighbors.

Let us also face some realities. It remains true that since at least the 1960s in the UK and since the 1970s in the USA, congregational participation has been in decline. In North America, mainline Protestant denominations initially experienced the greatest loss of members. However, since the turn of the millennium, most Evangelical Protestant and Roman Catholic bodies have followed suit.[1] In both the UK and US, this decline has prompted deep anxiety within denominational systems.

This anxiety is not unfounded. In the US context, "Research has consistently shown that every generation of adults is somewhat less religious than the generation that preceded it."[2] While less than 10 percent of the Silent Generation and fewer than 20 percent of Baby Boomers identify as "religiously unaffiliated," the percentage rises to nearly 30 percent for Millennials and more than a third for Generation Z.[3] It seems likely that this trend may continue among even younger generations, despite an encouraging recent uptick in church attendance by both Millennials and Gen Zers.

At the same time, God has not changed, and God's loving presence continues to be at work in the world. Over the course of two millennia, the Christian church in varied forms has proved remarkably resilient and been marked by a capacity to respond to social change and to renew herself. A key question that we are interested in is this: What does it mean and look like for local congregations to respond creatively to seismic changes today, newly attentive to what God is doing among us?

In response to the decline in attendance and financial giving, an entire industry has emerged to meet the demand for "congregational revitalization." The primary focus of this industry's programs and publications within Christian circles is "church growth," and they promote a revitalization recipe that combines bold leadership, compelling worship, inviting programs, and planting of new congregations.[4] Alongside marches a virtual army of consultants and proponents of particular models offering a prescription for success.

A different movement has also emerged. Rather than an attractional strategy of drawing people to one's congregation, this model calls on existing congregations to engage with their local communities attentively and with an open and receptive love. This has been dubbed the "missional church" movement in the Christian tradition. In a British context, "missional" was probably first used or at least popularized by theologian Lesslie Newbigin in the 1980s as a way to articulate the missionary nature of God and the call for the church to participate in the *Missio Dei*, God's mission.[5] The term gained traction in the US following publication of *Missional Church: A Vision for the Sending of the Church in North America*, in 1998.[6] As a response to congregational decline and the perceived liabilities of the church growth movement, the authors focused on the church's missional calling and urged that all members, "go out into the world and reflect the gospel in their surrounding communities."[7] In the UK, the publication in 2004 of the influential report *Mission-shaped Church* and the development of more pioneering approaches and "fresh expressions" of church had a similar thrust and impact.[8]

The calling to live out a faith community's values in the context of a specific local community cannot be reduced to one religious tradition. Yet we are speaking primarily from within our Christian tradition, and to its expression within mostly Anabaptist, Anglican, and other broadly Protestant denominations. For us, these are our own communities, the ones we have loved and worked with, and therefore the ones with which we are most familiar.

We believe that discerning a renewed missional calling is one vital pathway to the transformation of today's congregations. Something changes when a congregation stops looking in the mirror, steps outside the door, looks with new eyes, listens with fresh ears, and discerns how God is at work in the world well beyond the walls of a given congregation, and seeks to clarify her particular vocation within a local setting at this moment in history. The possibility of contributing to realizing God's realm, in partnership with the Holy Spirit, is reawakened.

Survey research indicates that younger generations have concerns that they feel an urgency to address. In our era, the top concerns for both Gen. Zers and Millennials in the US are climate change, poverty, and racial justice.[9] These concerns are echoed among younger people in the UK, especially regarding environmental care.[10] Therefore, congregations that demonstrate insufficient concern for these issues will likely be seen as irrelevant by these generations. At the same time, faith groups that only issue statements or verbally decry these realities will also be dismissed. What is desired is visible action, not words. Our conviction is that the action that typically most matters to people takes place in one's own community, in local neighborhoods.

This sets a priority on the "parish," the area served by a particular local congregation. While the term parish has typically been used by the historic Christian denominations, whether Roman Catholic, Orthodox, or Anglican (Episcopalian), to designate a bounded geographical area, this often has limitations which do not match realities on the ground. We will therefore use the term both in its traditional sense, and also to refer to the neighborhood(s) served by local congregations within a locality. When used this way, we are picturing resident-defined localities—the local communities that its people identify as "our neighborhood."[11] In this sense, the parish is the locus where a local congregation typically has most impact and most resonance.[12]

Why Us?

Both authors have spent decades providing congregational consulting and training services to predominantly Christian leaders and their congregations. David joined Mennonite Conciliation Service in Pennsylvania at the invitation of founder Ron Kraybill in 1986. Alastair co-founded Bridge Builders in 1995 at the London Mennonite Centre in England. Both of us learned that mediation and conflict resolution processes, while helpful in ameliorating the identified issues and bridging divided relationships, were inadequate to address the deeper issues of congregational culture. We therefore drew upon insights from the multi-disciplinary field of conflict studies, including systemic, power, and relational models—such as (Bowen) Family Systems Theory—to address the underlying patterns within congregational systems.[13]

Yet we both eventually concluded that something more was needed. David discovered in his practice and research that when a congregation shifts from an obsessive focus on internal issues to engage in new ways externally it experiences renewed energy, hope, and the release of the Holy Spirit. Here is how David describes his discovery:

> *In 2004, I surveyed 100 congregations in the American southwest regarding their experience of change and conflict in the previous five years. Only one change was negatively associated with conflict—meaning that it made conflict less likely. Congregations that started a "new community outreach" in the previous five years were less likely to report a significant conflict than similar congregations that did not.[14]*
>
> *Why would starting a project in the community make a congregation less prone to destructive conflict? My conclusion was that congregations with a primary internal focus will inevitably find much to quibble about, whereas externally focused congregations experience an internal alignment around a shared purpose.*
>
> *A healthy congregation celebrates marriages, dedicates babies, and commemorates the lives of the departed. Typically, every congregation must also attend to the administrative realities of balancing a budget, maintaining a facility, and making payroll. However, my conviction is that a congregation focused mainly on the needs of its members and the demands of its building and employees will eventually decline. For, "a congregation is the only association that exists for the benefit of those who are not its members," to paraphrase the Anglican archbishop William Temple.[15]*

Through my consulting work, I've noticed that unhealthy congregations, like unhealthy individuals, are self-absorbed. They fret about worship attendance and financial giving rather than focus on ministry. They develop a "scarcity mentality" and engage in turf wars over who will get what share of a steadily shrinking pie. They become oblivious to the community outside their own doors. By contrast, healthy congregations understand that they exist for the sake of their communities—both internally and externally. I've come to realize that healthy congregations look out the window—and head out the door.

Alastair's journey was different but marked by a similar shift in focus. Here is how he describes it:

When I launched Bridge Builders with others in the mid-1990s, my longing was to see the church more faithfully be the church.[16] I was convinced that if the church was going to proclaim a gospel of genuine good news to the wider world then we needed to live that out within our own midst. That meant finding better ways to handle our tensions, disagreements and conflicts, so that we better reflected the life of the community of heaven for which we are destined. I believed that we could only proclaim a gospel of peace with integrity, if we lived that out in our internal relationships.

Over the course of 20 years with Bridge Builders, my colleagues and I sought to make a contribution to changing the culture of how disagreement and conflict were handled in churches in Britain and Ireland.[17] In the second half of that time, my life was disrupted by a renewed sense of call to ordained ministry in the Church of England while doing doctoral research.[18] I strongly resisted that call, until overwhelmed by God showing me that I needed to heed the Spirit's promptings.

Shortly before being ordained in the Church of England in 2015, I stepped down from my role with Bridge Builders. The time seemed right to hand on the baton. I'd also had enough of working with internal church conflicts – although I had yet to fully admit and articulate that to myself.

I then worked at St Martin-in-the-Fields, in central London, for the practical stage of training for Anglican ministry. My experience at St Martin's exposed me to a breadth of missional engagement which continues to inspire me. I remain deeply shaped by the witness of the St Martin's community and by Sam Wells, their vicar, to the kindness and gentleness of God.

While expecting that ordination would lead onto a role working within the Church of England, I was surprised when nothing suitable emerged—despite testing it through one short-lived but painful "detour." Eventually, now unemployed, a conversation with Peter Price, a former bishop of Bath and Wells, brought hope. Peter named a renewed sense of call: that I should head up a new organization that I was in the process of launching, called Reconciliation Initiatives, working alongside Anglican churches in Britain and potentially beyond. This was a surprise, since it was only a variation on what I'd been doing prior to ordination. It also gave the opportunity to fulfill a longstanding yearning to explore how God's reconciling work might shape the church's missional engagement with the wider world, in her localities.

This led to the development of the Reconciling Mission *program, as one way to resource Anglican clergy, their local parishes and wider dioceses with options for engaging more deeply with their neighborhood(s), in more mutually respectful and empowering ways. This book is an attempt to explore and articulate that for a wider and ecumenical audience.*

Having worked as colleagues in delivering training programs in both the UK and the USA and having both written books focused on congregations and peacemaking, we were energized by the prospect of working on a new manuscript together. We hope that the comparative nature of our two different contexts brings a richness to what is offered, which can speak to leaders and congregational members in multiple contexts—perhaps not only in our home nations but also beyond.

Who Is Our Audience?

We write primarily for Christian clergy and lay leaders in local churches and larger regional contexts, including those at the leading edge of resourcing their people for missional engagement with local communities and neighborhoods. We expect that the book may also be useful for ministerial and lay leadership students, whether in residential or non-residential training. It is an exercise in practical theology intended to be useful to those in active ministry.

Why the Local?

One central premise of this book is that local congregations are the most important unit of action and analysis within the religious ecosystem.

Regional bodies and national denominations matter, but primarily to the extent to which they support, serve, and empower local congregations. Regional and national bodies in the USA and UK have been the locus of major conflict in recent decades, with the identified issue typically being different views relating to human sexuality and to gender. While such significant disagreements must be addressed, they have reduced the ability of such bodies to serve the felt needs of local congregations.

We believe that the local congregation situated in a unique local context is where the most important work of any religious tradition takes place. Each religious tradition has its own strengths and merits, and we recognize the value of some shared theological and organizational alignment. However, in an increasingly polarized age, where theological uniformity is no longer attainable—if it were ever desirable—we propose that the most significant affiliations are those that are joined in a particular local context. When Christians and those of other faiths find ways to work together for the good of a community, and when they join with other people of goodwill of no faith tradition, unity of *purpose* trumps the need for uniformity of *belief*.

When we as human beings work together with our neighbors for the flourishing of our local community to address issues of inequality or injustice that concern us, the need for uniformity of belief falls away. Our collaboration with one another, over what matters to us, will bind us together. No confessional statement, however robust, can achieve that. Hence, our primary focus is on the parish and its practices, on the local expression of the church.

Why Coalitions?

We will explore the outreach work of individual congregations. However, we will also consider the impact of congregational and organizational coalitions or partnerships, and what they can contribute to a community. That is because the ability of any single congregation to achieve transformational change in a neighborhood or community is circumscribed. Congregational and organizational coalitions, by contrast, have a demonstrated track record of bringing about transformational change.

The work of coalition-building is distinct from that of offering essential services, advocating for the disadvantaged, or forming a community development organization. The work of coalition-building involves patient attention to relationships, to the interests of each participating group, and to the underlying needs of community members. It is relatively easy for a single congregation to establish a food pantry, advocate for affordable housing, or form a separate non-profit organization. However, such steps may do relatively little to change systemic challenges, inequalities and injustices, which can be better impacted through wider collaboration.

Successful collaboration requires a willingness to be changed as much as to work for change. It is precisely that openness to being changed which produces genuine change in our neighborhoods and communities. Unless a critical mass within a local congregation is willing to be changed, we should not anticipate any significant change within our surrounding community.

What Is Reconciling Mission?

Reconciling Mission is multiple things.

- Reconciling mission is foremost a way of referring to God's reconciling work in the world, and our invitation to join in with this, in what the apostle Paul speaks of as God reconciling the world to God's self, through Christ. (2 Cor. 5:18)
- *Reconciling Mission* is the title of an 18-month learning and development program which equips small groups of ordained church leaders—sponsored by a regional team—to resource local congregations for deeper engagement with their neighbors and local context, with the aim of contributing to greater reconciliation in society.[19]
- The name also hints at the need for our approaches to the Christian missional task to be reconciled, since many historic approaches are marred with imperialist pretentions, violence, and the domination of indigenous peoples. The reality is that these still influence and can overshadow how congregations and Christian agencies approach missional engagement and think about "mission."

While referring to all three of these in our book title, we also believe that there is value in exploring reconciliation as a reference paradigm for the church's missional engagement with local communities. This is because it is easy to over-focus on the church, and to miss a correcting emphasis on God's reign. When we focus on contributing to more of God's realm being realized here on earth, anxieties about the church can fall away—or at least can be brought back into needed perspective.

At the same time, we are conscious of the misuse of the concept of reconciliation in the Christian theological tradition, as articulated by Willie James Jennings, amongst others.[20] The danger is that a focus on reconciliation can be used to promote harmony at the cost of addressing issues of inequality and injustice. Hence, the journey towards reconciliation offered in the theoretical framework engaged with and modelled in the case studies, is therefore one of seeking greater social equality and justice as signs of the inbreaking of God's realm. There can be no genuine reconciliation without justice.

In our opening chapter, we will therefore offer some "route maps" to help local congregations locate themselves and their missional journeys. Chapter 1 begins with setting out a theoretical framework which will be used as a dialogue partner in each of our subsequent chapters. This is a framework or route map employed within the *Reconciling Mission* program, derived from the wider field of peacebuilding and conflict transformation. It will enable us to identify where each community engagement approach appears to sit on a journey towards greater social reconciliation and justice, as a contribution to seeing more of God's reign realized here on earth. While remembering that this will only be partially experienced while we live in this in-between season: between Christ's initial incarnation and his final coming which will usher in the fulfillment of all that God has in store for humanity and creation, into eternity.[21]

The opening chapter therefore goes on to explore two further route maps, key foundational stories within the Biblical canon: the story of Moses's journey with Israel, set out in the book of Exodus; and Jesus's journey with Israel, captured through the four lenses of the gospel writers, with a particular focus here on Mark's account. A distinctive feature of both of these journeys is that the routes integrate what can be described as significant "detours." These detours are deviations from the route that we might expect the characters to take in fulfilling their destinies. The experience of detours proves to have an intriguing resonance as we explore the case studies set out in the subsequent chapters.

What Do We Mean?

We use a couple of technical terms in this book. Here briefly is what we mean by these:

Asset-Based Community Development (ABCD): Asset-Based Community Development "is a bottom-up way of working with communities that focuses on community strengths and assets rather than on deficits and problems."[22]

Congregation-Based Community Organizing (CBCO): Congregation-Based Community Organization "describes a wide variety of efforts to empower residents in a local area to participate in civic life or governmental affairs."[23]

Where Are We Going?

In broad terms this book is an exercise in practical theology, drawing on qualitative research in the form of interviews with case studies. We write from our locations in differing societies, the United Kingdom and the United States, about diverse models of community engagement. We seek to bring together different but complementary streams that have emerged from a similar impulse—to engage congregations in their local context. We will endeavor to highlight some distinctive developments that have emerged in both American and European contexts, informed by the chosen case studies. Our aim is to offer a constructive way forward for the current missional challenge facing Christian congregations, in both Britain and the States, and potentially beyond.

In our concluding chapter, we will identify key threads and themes of the different approaches explored. At this stage, it is worth noting three core elements. The approaches are all:

1 *Locally-Rooted*: The general idea of the "parish" is central: a gathered congregation or congregations located within a particular local community and context.[24]
2 *Asset-Based*: All of the case studies recognize that every local community is composed of individuals and organizations with "assets," that is gifts, passions, strengths and skills, as well as significant needs.

3 *Bridge-Building*: The goal of bridging divisions, addressing hurts, transforming conflict, and strengthening relationships and the social fabric of a local community, including addressing systemic challenges, are either implicit or explicit within each approach.

In summary then:

Chapter 1 lays out route maps in the form of theoretical and theological frameworks for Reconciling Mission, including two foundational Biblical narratives, given shape through the lives and journeys of Moses and Jesus.

Chapters 2 through 6 explore case studies from English and American contexts, ranging from sparsely rural to large urban communities.

Chapter 7, the concluding chapter, distills insights, notes commonalities and distinctives, and identifies useful aspects of the Reconciling Mission framework.

We finish by pointing to a pathway for congregations and their leaders who desire to deepen the journey of community engagement. We believe that local congregations need their communities as much as communities need their congregations. Congregations may begin a process of community engagement by seeking to address core human needs—such as food, clothing, shelter, transportation, or childcare. As awareness of deeper structural issues surfaces, congregations can shift from "doing to" or "doing for" into "acting with" and "working by"—a shift to mutual interdependence.[25]

It is in this deeper partnership that genuine mutuality emerges, and where a congregation discovers the multiple gifts in the broader community that before were unrecognized or underappreciated. As a congregation listens *to* its community, learns *from* its community, and acts *with* its community, mutual transformation results. Congregations can be transformed and potentially revitalized through community engagement, and local communities can be restored and more reconciled. Our diverse case studies put flesh on this claim.

While not immediately obvious, a key starting place is likely to be a renewed sense of vocation, of discerning God's particular calling for our local congregation, and our contribution to the neighborhood and community within which we are located, based on a deeper love for the locality and our neighbors, in order to see a flourishing of the "common good."[26] As we learn to listen more deeply to the Holy Spirit, we will listen more closely to our neighbors, in the journey of stepping over the congregation's thresholds.[27]

By the end of this book, we hope that our readers will be inspired to prompt their churches into deeper community engagement, be encouraged that there is hope for their neighborhood, and be more confident that they can explore and work with their neighbors to see more of God's realm realized in their local context.

1 Big Picture and Foundational Stories

This chapter offers a distinctive framework for thinking about the church's missional engagement with local neighborhood and community. It also explores two foundational Biblical stories and how they connect with and extend this framework. The chapter includes simple line drawings which give one image to help the reader remember that stage of the journey.[1]

There is nothing so practical as good theory, as this author has noted elsewhere.[2] With an extended background in practical peacemaking, in 2018 I (Alastair) turned to a theoretical model from an English Quaker peacemaker, Adam Curle, as a resource for thinking about the church's missional engagement with our neighbors.[3] Curle's model has been fruitfully applied to international peacebuilding by influential practitioners such as John Paul Lederach.[4] Why might it be relevant to the church's outreach? One reason is that Curle charts a journey from conflictual and unjust relationships to sustainably just and peaceful ones. Curle's destination is a way of describing the coming kingdom of heaven, or picturing God's reign here on earth. If we want to see God's reign realized, it helps to conceive what it looks like, practically. Without a clear sense of our destination, we are unlikely to end up there. To paraphrase Seneca, if we do not know which port we are heading for in our ship—a classic metaphor for the church—we will not know which wind to set our sails to.

Crucially, it also helps to recognize the stages of the journey that we may need to pass through in order to reach the destination. Our corporate missional journeys, much like our personal ones, are rarely linear or straightforward. They may at times include spiraling backwards. Knowing which staging posts to look out for along the way can help us discern where we are on the journey, and what to attend to as we attempt to move closer to our destination.

Further, it helps to recognize the dynamics of the forces at play. Curle's model intersects three dimensions: the relative balance of power of the parties involved, their awareness and sense of conflict, and the movement towards more peaceful relations. To continue the metaphor, when setting sail on a long journey, it will help to understand the winds and ocean currents, the progression of the seasons and how to read the stars.

Reconciling Mission: A Reference Framework

Inspired by Curle, I propose that there are potentially five distinct stages on a missional journey of seeing more of God's reign realized here on earth. These are:

1 Meeting basic human needs
2 Raising awareness of injustice
3 Challenging the system
4 Transforming systems
5 Realizing more of God's reign

In practice, the stages can overlap or bridge different elements, with the fifth being more of a description of the destination than a separate stage. Let us unpack each in turn.

Image 1.1 Meeting Basic Human Needs

Meeting Basic Human Needs

In thinking about engagement with neighbors, a natural starting place for many churches will be to find a way to respond to felt or perceived needs. Are local families going without enough to eat? Let us offer them food. Are there people on our streets without a home? Let us provide shelter for them. Are parents with young children or older members of our community feeling lonely and isolated? Let us offer them hospitality which provides company and social interaction.

In the UK in recent years there has been a proliferation of churches involved in local food banks, often hosted within a church building, with church members and other volunteers distributing free food to their needy neighbors. This activity accelerated following the disruptions of the Covid-19 pandemic, and the energy crisis brought on by the invasive war in Ukraine. Hundreds of thousands of hungry people, including many children, have been fed through these food banks.[5] It is a sign of the times featuring increasing social inequalities that so many people are struggling to make ends meet in one of the wealthiest countries on earth.

At one level, it is clearly admirable that Christian people have stepped up to respond. Whether motivated by human compassion or by the challenge of Jesus, that "just as you did it to one of the least of these …, you did it to me" (Mt 25:40), Christians often have the sense that this is the right thing to do. Such charitable projects offer an avenue to channel people's goodwill and their desire to share essentials with others in need. As Andrew Rumsey has illustrated, in an English context this links into a historical pattern which was a root of the parish system: of providing aid for one's impoverished neighbors.[6] Furthermore, such service provision has the potential to be a route into building deeper relationships with neighbors. So, what is not to like?

Curle's model prompts us to think about power dynamics. One risk is that our charitable actions can feed our unacknowledged paternalistic instincts, being more about us feeling good about ourselves. Our actions can potentially also create unhealthy dependency and further disempower those we want to help. In a striking dialogue with a 19th-century critique by Oscar Wilde, Sam Wells highlights the real dangers of charitable action.[7] The well-intentioned "remedies" of admirable people "do not cure the disease: they merely prolong it. Indeed, their remedies are part of the disease."[8] In other words, if our supposedly worthy and altruistic actions serve to reinforce the status quo, they become part of the problem, not part of the solution.

Prior to the Covid-19 pandemic, significant numbers of local churches banded together to respond to rising homelessness in Britain, especially during the harsh winter months from November to February. A classic response was to establish a winter night shelter for local homeless people, with seven churches in an area each hosting on different nights. This provided a place of shelter every night of the week, without a heavy burden falling on a single church. A group of churches in the London Borough of Haringey in north London organized one such rotation. A hot evening meal and cooked breakfast were provided, access to a shower, and a mattress and bedding in a warm, dry space. Friendly conversation was offered over the table, and the opportunity to play games and have some fun. A large team was required from each church to deliver this, and there was much that was good about it.

However, there were troubling aspects. There was an enforced peripatetic existence for the homeless people. There was also a maintenance of strict boundaries. So, for example, the homeless people were not allowed to help with the cooking, serving, or clearing away at mealtimes. This demarcated who was a client and who was delivering the service. It failed to empower the homeless people to participate and contribute as peers with the volunteers.

This is not to suggest that the local church and her members abandon all charitable acts. Everyday acts of kindness should often be welcomed. Further, working to address a local need has every chance of being an important starting place for a congregation in learning to "journey out," especially if they have a history of being overly inward-looking.[9] However, as Curle's framework and theologian Ann Morisy both remind us, we will need to go beyond helping to meet others' basic needs if we are to move faithfully towards offering a richer foretaste of the heavenly banquet. Something significant needs to shift in the power and relational dynamics.

Image 1.2 Raising Awareness of Injustice

Raising Awareness of Injustice

The Brazilian adult educator, Paulo Freire, has highlighted the significance of "conscientization": the raising of people's awareness and understanding of the nature and outworking of injustice.[10] It is one thing to feed the hungry. It is another to grapple with why people are going hungry. For many of us, it is often harder and more uncomfortable to grasp *why* people are experiencing inequality or injustice, than simply to be involved in trying to meet a real need.

Campaigning organizations recognize the importance of the educational task in galvanizing people to act. This is illustrated by the work of the Clewer Initiative, a Church of England project. Clewer exists "to raise awareness and mobilize the Church and communities to take action against modern slavery, to promote victim identification and to provide victim care and support."[11] The Clewer Initiative understands that raising awareness is a critical step in tackling modern-day slavery. One aspect is enabling people to realize that such slavery is often hidden in plain sight; and then helping people to notice potential signs of vulnerable people being exploited by others. Hence Clewer's campaign banner of "we see you," expressing their goal of making victims visible. An example is pop-up hand car washes, where vulnerable migrants are forced to work long hours, for little or no pay, under threat of violence. An app installed on one's cell phone helps people to look for signs and then to take action to report questionable activity to a local authority.

For one parish in the north of England, engaging with the Clewer Initiative's resources led them onto exploring the challenges facing refugees and immigrants without legal permission to remain in the UK.[12] Some in their parish then followed up with a visit to The Jungle, near Calais in northern France. This was a self-established refugee camp that existed for two years from 2015, until cleared and bulldozed by the French police.[13] The effect of this visit was transformational for these parishioners in raising their awareness and understanding.

My own organization, Reconciliation Initiatives, is involved in awareness-raising work in the racial justice arena. We offer a four-month program called *Being White*, facilitated by and aimed at those who are racialized as white.[14] This seeks to explore white identity and raise white church leaders' awareness of the systemic and institutional nature of racism in English society, including inside the church. It explores the normativity of "whiteness" and the benefits that those of us who are white typically and unthinkingly enjoy in our context, relative to many of our black and brown brothers and sisters.[15] The program challenges those of us who are white to shoulder our responsibilities in the work of dismantling systemic and institutional racism, and thus to do the work that is ours to do. Rather than looking to people of color—as so often in the past—to do the heavy lifting for us. The program seeks to resource church leaders to be proactively anti-racist, and to support them in embracing, integrating, and celebrating greater racial diversity as a joyful aspect of the kingdom of heaven, here on earth.

Such limited preparatory work needs to go hand-in-hand with wider work of addressing racial justice within a diocese or judicatory. This would include prioritizing and listening to the lived experience of people of global majority heritage; and developing inter-cultural work that promotes mutual respect and understanding. Nevertheless, within the predominantly white Church of England, often unconsciously caught up in a culture of whiteness, it is necessary awareness-raising work which can help our leaders and churches towards realizing more of God's reign. This can move us closer towards Revelation's eschatological vision of people of every nation, tribal group, and tongue worshipping God together with mutual respect and enjoyment. (Rev 7:9)

Raising awareness of injustice is a second stage on the missional journey we are charting. It matters because the issues contributing to inequity are often complex and need deeper understanding if we are to find a way to address them effectively. Otherwise, the danger is that we blunder along with well-intentioned but ill-informed boots. However, it is not the place to stop. Curle's model reminds us that the power dynamics here often remain unequal, and there can be a lack of genuine mutuality. The journey needs to continue forwards with concrete steps of protest and action.

Challenging the System

Human systems tend towards maintaining things the way they are, as Murray Bowen observed.[16] Finding ways to disrupt such systems is therefore rarely easy. It is also unlikely to come about without a struggle. This stage in the journey typically involves protesting that how things are currently working in our society are not fair, right, or adequate to address the issues being faced. When this protest builds momentum, we notice a movement across a society, or even globally. The year 2019 saw such a movement in relation to the environmental crisis facing our world. This was catalyzed by individuals

Image 1.3 Challenging the System

like the young Swedish girl, Greta Thunberg, who began her school strikes a year earlier. In the UK, we saw widespread climate protests across the country. Some of these led to the closure of key thoroughfare streets in our capital city, attracting major media interest. Christians joined in these protests, either as part of secular associations such as Extinction Rebellion, or as part of faith groups such as Christian Climate Action, "a prayerful community of Christians supporting each other to take meaningful action in the face of imminent and catastrophic anthropogenic climate breakdown."[17]

In the protests of 2019 and subsequent years, ordinary people collaborated to demand that concrete action be taken by their governments to address global warming and environmental damage caused by human activity.[18] While deniers remain, these protests and campaigning—reinforced by people experiencing more extreme weather events—mean that it is now hard for anyone to be unaware of the environmental crisis facing our planet.

One way that local churches in England and Wales have practically responded to this movement is through entering into the Eco Church scheme, a project of A Rocha.[19] One vicar in the Diocese of Lincoln shared this story about how his parish engaged with the scheme:

> *In 2021, as we emerged from the Covid-19 restrictions, one of our lay leaders, Keith Farmery, investigated Eco Awards and caught a vision for how the parish of All Saints, New Brumby, might participate. Keith invited congregation members to meet and explore the idea. After initial concerns were expressed about the work involved, people saw the benefits of contributing to improving the local environment. They realized that achieving the Bronze Award was within their reach; and saw the opportunity to involve other people in the neighborhood.*
>
> *With the help of youth from local uniformed organizations, they made bird feeders, bird boxes and bug hotels for placing in the churchyard; and they planted wildflowers. The congregation implemented a plan for recycling waste, and for using more sustainable kitchen and cleaning products. The lighting in the church hall needed replacement. So, a decision was taken by the church council to replace this with energy efficient fittings and luminaires.*
>
> *Local businesses and neighbors were encouraged to get involved by supplying materials for the bird feeders and boxes, the bug hotels, and in sourcing the wildflower seeds. Further, they supplied and installed the light fittings and fixtures at a reduced cost. Other members of the community*

helped by clearing the churchyard for the wildflower planting, and mounting the feeders, boxes and hotels. It became a genuine community project. After a few months the parish achieved the Eco Church Bronze Award; and within a year had taken further steps and achieved the Silver Award – one of only four churches in the Diocese of Lincoln so far to do so. The parish is now working towards the Gold Award and exploring how to further involve the local community. Congregation members have been hugely encouraged that they could act together to improve the local environment – and work with their neighbors in doing so.[20]

Sometimes challenging the system can be an even quieter affair, and part of a movement that attracts less media attention. One impact of the viral pandemic, from 2020 onwards, has been a rise in mental health challenges faced by many, including young people. Indeed, the World Health Organization now recognizes loneliness, which is at the root of many mental difficulties, as "a pressing global health threat."[21] Alongside this health crisis has been a "talking revolution," as termed by a Fellow of the Royal Society of Arts (RSA).[22] This is a quiet revolution of citizen-led initiatives offering listening services outside the formal health system. Through the early months of the pandemic, in conversation with others, one parish priest discerned a need for this locally.[23] In collaboration with a medical practice and a group of lay people, they set up a lay-led listening service. Rather than leaving it up to over-stretched healthcare professionals and expecting the under-resourced National Health Service to meet the need, this group took the initiative to offer a service to their local community. They challenged the healthcare system that people had come to rely on since 1945. As the RSA Fellow noted, this is part of a wider—if less organized—movement empowering ordinary people to play a part in improving their neighbors' wellbeing, instead of leaving it to professionals. Momentum has now built to such an extent that it possible to talk of creating a neighborhood health service.[24]

One difficulty of challenging the system through protest is that it takes significant work to translate protest into practical action, and still more to bring about changes in government and intergovernmental policy. Because of the power imbalances, protest can be hard to sustain over time, as individuals run out of energy and the *status quo* reasserts itself. To move onto the next stage of the missional journey, a way needs to be found to transform systems.

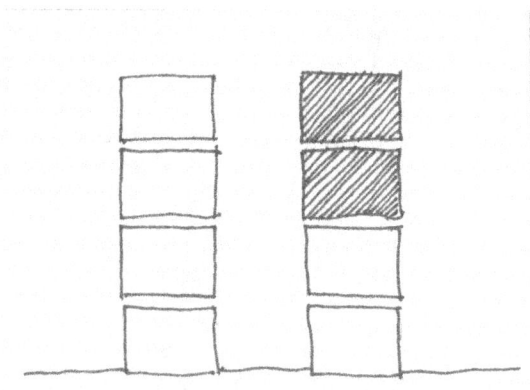

Image 1.4 Transforming Systems

Transforming Systems

This stage is about changing the nature of the interactions in a community—or potentially even within a nation—and achieving a more balanced and equitable relationship. It may be easier to notice this stage when it happens at a national level. When a group of people, such as women, are finally given the vote or given the freedom to be considered for an episcopal role; or when another group of people, such as people of color, are given the opportunity to vote, or be educated equally with others, then it is evident that a substantive change, a rebalancing in the power dynamics has happened.

Sometimes, it may be less easy to notice such change at a local level. One illustration comes from the work of St Mary's Centre for Peace and Reconciliation in Luton, England. This center was founded in 2009 by Peter Adams, a man with a vision for peacemaking in his local community. He aimed to understand, engage, and challenge the activity of street-based right-wing racist and anti-Islamic movements within the town.[25] Luton is one of the most ethnically diverse communities in the UK: over half of the residents are of a different ethnicity than white.[26] Luton is also the home of Stephen Lennon, better known by his pseudonym as "Tommy Robinson."[27] In response to a protest by a small but extreme Islamic group, Robinson co-founded the English Defence League (EDL) in 2009. This group organized large demonstrations on Luton's streets, most notably in 2011 and 2012. Their marches were an attempt to divide the community along racial lines, promote the supremacy of white people, and isolate people from UK ethnic minorities.

In response, Peter Adams and his friends organized local church leaders and groups to provide a peacebuilding presence. They worked at building relationships with those of other faith traditions, especially the Muslim community targeted by the EDL. Through being part of community-cohesion groups, together they worked closely with the police—a novelty for leaders in the Islamic community—to ensure that the EDL's marches were fairly and firmly policed. This prevented EDL protesters from taking provocative routes through the town.

At the heart of this process, which has continued into the present, has been enabling people of different faith traditions and ethnicities to understand one another and act together. It has enabled them to find ways to stand together in the face of those wanting to divide the community. A decade later, it led one BBC reporter to conclude that the process had enabled the people of Luton to beat the extremists and foil their divisive efforts.[28]

This story illustrates a shift in power dynamics within a local community. For a season, those on the extremes—both Islamic fundamentalists and English nationalists—got the attention and set the local tone for Luton. They gave the town a poor reputation. The intentional work of Peter Adams, his Muslim friend Rehana Faisal, and a team of their respective colleagues helped to empower the silent voices of the quiet majority in the middle ground. They were able to stand together in changing the culture of a community. Importantly, they have recognized that it takes ongoing, long-term work for the change to be consolidated: sustaining relationships and remaining in dialogue with neighbors who are different to themselves.[29]

Effecting systemic transformation typically takes long-term commitment and collaborative action. It often involves an extended struggle with major setbacks, before achieving the desired change. Ask those who were part of the civil rights movement in the USA in the 1950s and 1960s; or those in the anti-apartheid movement in South Africa over many decades before the democratic elections of 1994. This also applies at a local level, as shown by the work of St Mary's Centre for Peace and Reconciliation. It takes a commitment to relationship-building, collaborative-working and coalition-forming over the long haul.

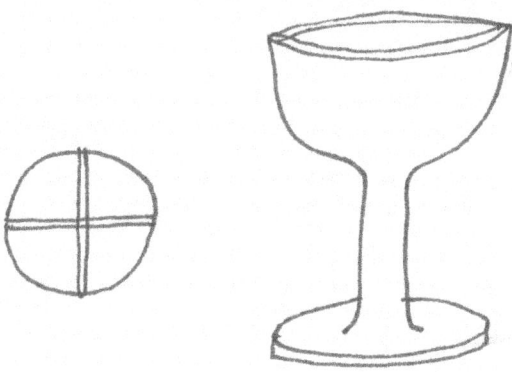

Image 1.5 Realizing More of God's Reign

Realizing More of God's Reign

The missional journey described above is moving us closer to experiencing a foretaste of heaven here on earth: realizing more of God's reign. As widely recognized by theologians, we live in an in-between season: between Christ's first coming, which has seen a breaking-in of God's kingdom, and his second, which will usher in the fulfillment of all that God has in store for humanity and creation, into eternity.[30] Therefore, this side of the grave we will never fully experience God's reign. However, the promise of Jesus is that we can experience a foretaste. With his arrival, and through the ongoing work of the Holy Spirit, Jesus asserts that "the kingdom of God is among you." (Lk 17:21) When we have more just and equal interactions among neighbors in which each person's voice is heard, each one is invited to participate, and each person's contribution is valued and cherished, then we have a taste of the heaven that is to come and are "living God's future now."[31] We are closer to our destination, the final reconciliation that God is bringing.

Conclusion

One benefit of Adam Curle's model is that it helps a missional-minded church move beyond thinking about addressing basic needs. Addressing such needs can be a vital starting place. However, it is often where many churches stop in their missional outreach. The model highlights the importance of taking

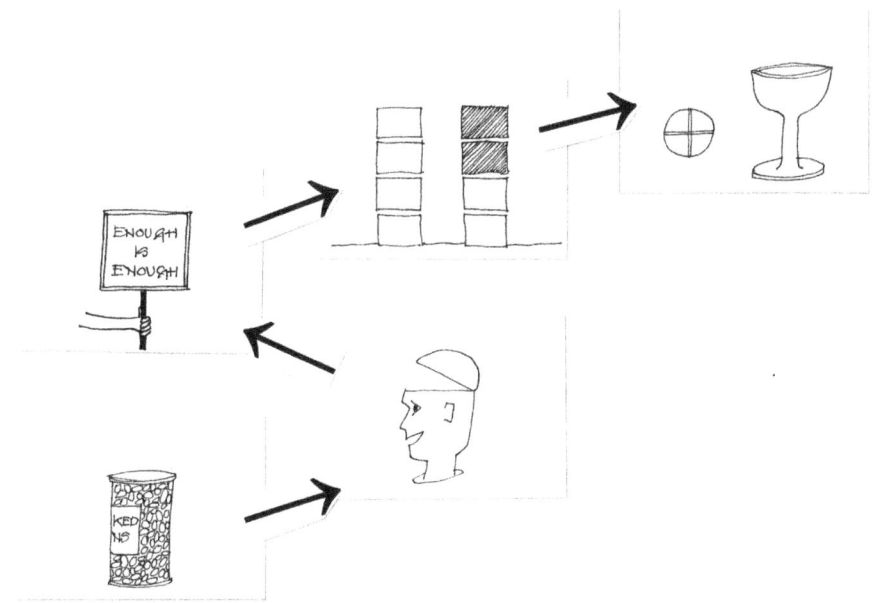

Image 1.6 Theoretical Framework

account of the power dynamics, and of noticing the requirement to engage in a struggle and to contribute to action which moves us closer towards a greater foretaste of the heavenly banquet. This journey is therefore likely to be contested, conflictual, and uncomfortable, which may be why many churches avoid it.

Nevertheless, Curle's framework has limitations. For example, Curle is not seeking to give a sufficient description of the key ingredients of a heavenly-tinged life, as we are describing it. Sam Wells's conceptualization of eight key features of this life is therefore helpful.[32] Wells sees that this life will be marked by: being more fully *present* to one another; being more *attentive* to others; being able to enter into the *mystery* of life and death; being able to *delight* in the world and other people; experiencing the full *participation* of everyone; working together in *partnership* with others; entering fully into the *enjoyment* of one another and the created world; and gaining a sense of God's *glory*, revealed most fully in Jesus. These eight dimensions can usefully be employed as markers of the heavenly life. They also offer one way of testing whether the life that we consider we are experiencing bears a genuinely heavenly hallmark, a sign of God's reign.

Foundational Stories

In this section we explore two foundational stories from the Biblical canon, those of Moses and Jesus. These two stories have defined and shaped the people of God in their understanding of themselves: Moses, for the people of Israel, and subsequently for Christians; and Jesus, most centrally for the entire Christian church. We notice a striking correspondence between both narratives with the journey named in Adam Curle's framework.

We also discover that there are significant "detours" in both narratives. These are ways in which the primary character's journey seems to deviate from the route that we might expect in fulfilling their destinies. In applying Curle's framework, peacebuilding practitioners are clear that the path is rarely linear and can cycle back on itself.[33] Detours in these foundational narratives are therefore important to notice as a reminder that our local missional journeys are unlikely to be linear. We may well meet roadblocks and travel down detours. However, in God's gracious economy these detours can be reintegrated into the story. Often—and surprisingly—in ways which prove crucial to the story's later development.

Foundational Story 1: Moses's Journey with Israel

The defining story of God's originally chosen people, of Israel, is the story of Moses: his journey and the Israelites' exodus from Egypt and release from enslavement to Pharoah and the Egyptian empire. With Curle's framework in mind, we can identify five stages in the story, as follows:

1 Being Raised in Pharaoh's House
　Detour: Killing an Egyptian
2 Learning in Midian
3 Confronting Pharaoh
4 Crossing the Red Sea
5 Journeying towards the Promised Land

Let us explore each stage.

Image 1.7 Being Raised in Pharaoh's House

Being Raised in Pharaoh's House

Out of fear of being overrun by an immigrant people—the Israelites—Pharaoh appoints taskmasters to "oppress them with forced labor." (Ex 1:11–14) Not content with making life impossibly hard for the Israelites, Pharaoh commands the Hebrew midwives to kill all new male infants upon delivery. When this fails, he orders his own people to cast such infants into the river Nile. (Ex 1:15–22) In response, one Hebrew mother first hides her son, then places him in a floating basket at a strategic place on the river, among the reeds. (Ex 2:1–4) The child is found by Pharaoh's daughter when she comes to bathe—presumably a daily ritual observed by the mother. Pharaoh's daughter discovers the infant and "took pity on him." (Ex 2:6) Deducing his heritage, she has him "fostered" by a Hebrew woman, thanks to the child's older sister; a woman who just happens to be the child's mother.[34] (Ex 2:6–9) After weaning the infant, the Hebrew mother surrenders him up to be adopted by Pharaoh's daughter, who names him "Moses" (Mosheh), "because … I drew him out of the water." (Ex 2:10) Moses is then raised in Pharaoh's house.

Judging from the next chapter in his story it appears that Moses somehow learns of his Hebrew heritage. However, as the adopted son of Pharaoh's daughter, he is raised and inculcated in all the ways of Pharoah's court. Throughout his childhood, Moses thus has a dual existence. It was likely an internally conflictual one as both an insider and an outsider. A life both *of* his adoptive family and different from it.

The issue at Moses's birth is survival, with the threat of death hanging over him. By claiming the child as her own son, Pharoah's daughter provides protection and nourishment for the boy—and subverts her father's command. She arranges for the boy's basic human needs to be met, ensuring that he can not only survive but thrive under her care. We also note that Moses's infancy experience prefigures the saving of his whole nation "out of the water."

Detour: Killing an Egyptian

Once he reaches adulthood, Moses's identification with his "kinsfolk" overrides his allegiance to Pharoah's family. (Ex 2:11–13) Enraged at the treatment of "his people," he takes matters into his own hands, and kills an Egyptian taskmaster. This action, driven by a powerful emotional reaction, is presumably fueled by anger pent up throughout his upbringing. It is pointless, as it will make no dent in the Egyptian empire's machinery. It also fails to arouse approval from his fellow Hebrews. They reveal that his action—which he had tried to hide—is public knowledge. (Ex 2:12–14) He is known to be a murderer. Once Pharaoh learns of it, he wants Moses dead. (Ex 2:15)

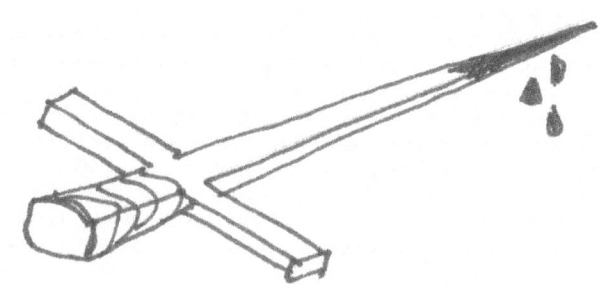

Image 1.8 Killing an Egyptian

This is a detour in Moses's story on at least two counts. It deviates from any path that the God of Israel would have chosen for him. The Hebrew tradition outlawed murder, as Moses himself would later reveal to the people. (Ex 20:13) Being a member of Pharaoh's household, Moses was uniquely placed to mediate and influence Pharoah for the good of the Israelites. One could argue that the God of Israel had placed him there. Moses forgoes the opportunity to come to his people's aid in a more skillful, diplomatic, and strategic way. Instead, through hot-headed action, he is forced to flee. He must leave the country, and the center of the empire, to escape Pharoah's wrath.

Learning in Midian

Moses flees Egypt and goes to the land of Midian.[35] This was—and remains—a desert. This must have been disorienting and dislocating for Moses. He had been raised in the heart of the Egyptian court. In British terms, this would have been like being brought up in the Prime Minister's residence in Downing Street in central London. Being relocated to Midian would have been like moving to Sutherland in Scotland, a remote area of Britain.[36] In Pharaoh's house, Moses had been at the center of societal power. Now, a refugee with a criminal past, he finds himself herding sheep in the wilderness, in an alien land. (Ex 2:15b–22) Was this what God wanted for him?

Image 1.9 Learning in Midian

Moses's time in Midian enables God to educate him afresh. He learns intimacy in human relationships, through marriage to Zipporah, through working for his father-in-law, Jethro, and through becoming a father. As importantly, Moses learns to listen to God. This is encapsulated by the dialogue with God at Horeb, after noticing the blazing bush which was not consumed. When he listens, Moses discovers that God has been attentive to the people of Israel. God has observed their misery and listened to their cry at how they are oppressed.

Moses also learns that God has a plan: "I will send you to Pharaoh to bring my people, the Israelites, out of Egypt." (Ex 3:10) Despite Moses's intense doubt and resistance, God commissions him for his life's next stage. It involves returning to Egypt, to Pharaoh and the center of power, and demanding the release of God's people from the empire. God also reassures Moses that, "all those who are seeking your life are dead." (Ex 4:19) Moses will not have to account for his criminal past.

Moses's time in Midian proves a re-education. Through listening, Moses discovers that God is fully aware of the oppression of the Israelites and has a plan to rescue them. A plan in which Moses is central.

Image 1.10 Confronting Pharaoh

Confronting Pharaoh

Despite his misgivings, but aided by his brother, Moses gathers the elders of Israel together and persuades them that God "had given heed to the Israelites and … had seen their misery." This prompts all the Israelite people to bow down and worship. (Ex 4:27–31) Accompanied by Aaron, Moses then goes to Pharaoh with a message from the God of Israel to, "Let my people go."

This message is not well received. Pharaoh responds, "Who is the LORD, that I should heed him and let Israel go? I do not know the LORD, and I will not let Israel go." (Ex 5:1–2) Repeatedly, Pharaoh refuses to listen, despite the terrible plague events which befall his people. (Ex 7–11) After each plague Pharaoh initially indicates that he *will* let the people go; but immediately reneges on his undertaking once Moses has prayed for the plague's removal. Until a final devastating plague results in the death of all the firstborn in Egypt, both human and animal, excepting the firstborn of the Israelites. Whereupon Pharaoh pleads with Moses, "Rise up, go away from my people, both you and the Israelites … be gone." Brazenly adding, "And bring a blessing on me too!" (Ex 12:31–32) At last, the Israelites can leave, along with donations given by their Egyptian neighbors, who now long to see the back of them.

Systems of enslavement are deeply embedded in the economic systems of empires. They may be formalized as chattel slavery, as during the dominance of the British Empire in the 18th and 19th centuries; or they may be structured in through the mass exploitation of poor workers, as in the 20th-century capitalist system of American and Western European dominance. Changing such systems does not happen without a huge struggle. It should therefore be no surprise that freeing the Israelites was costly; or that Pharaoh's Egyptian empire stubbornly resisted for so long. Freedom only came through huge perseverance by Moses and Aaron to continue challenging the system. This also in the face of the Israelites' understandable lack of faith, "because of their broken spirit and their cruel slavery." (Ex 6:9)

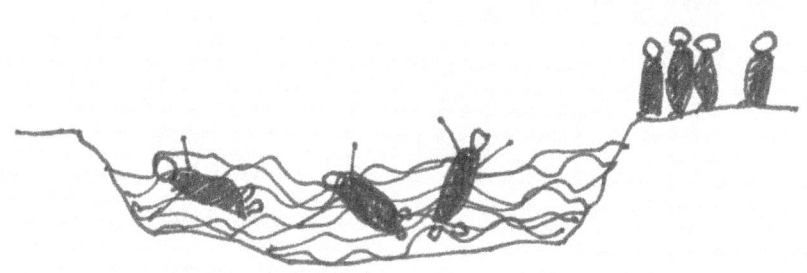

Image 1.11 Crossing the Red Sea

Crossing the Red Sea

After the Israelites have left the Egyptian center, Pharaoh has yet another change of heart: "What have we done, letting Israel leave our service?" (Ex 14:6) The exodus of their free labor force causes Pharaoh and his entourage to panic. They send the empire's full military might in pursuit. By this time the Israelites have reached the sea. Now they find themselves hemmed in by Pharaoh's forces. The Israelites' raise their voices against Moses: "Was it because there were no graves in Egypt that you have taken us away to die in the wilderness?" (Ex 14:11) Moses calls the people not to be afraid and to stand firm, for: "The Lord will fight for you, and you have only to keep still." (Ex 14:14) Not literally still, because they next must walk through two great walls of water, when God creates a dry pathway through the sea during the night. (Ex 14:21–22)

They are pursued by the Egyptian military. However, once the Israelites have passed safely through, God instructs Moses to stretch out his hand, "and at dawn the sea returned to its normal depth," swallowing up "the entire army of Pharaoh." (Ex 14:26–28) The canonic writer sums up the outcome: "Thus the LORD saved Israel that day from the Egyptians; and Israel saw the Egyptians dead on the seashore." A fundamental and permanent change in the power dynamics had happened. The military might of the empire is undone. The Israelites are free to journey on without fear of their previous oppressors. Free to learn together what it means to love God and their neighbor.

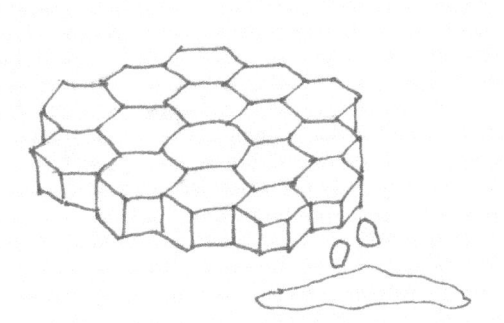

Image 1.12 Journeying towards the Promised Land

Journeying towards the Promised Land

The Israelites are freed from their heavy yoke of slavery. However, they still have much to learn. They struggle to embrace their dependency on God and to trust in God's provision: witness the story of the manna, in Exodus 16. Like anyone freed from an extended time of imprisonment, they faced a huge number of unexpected choices. What are they to do with their freedom? God does not leave them floundering but offers 10 guiding words or commandments. (Ex 20:1–17) These key words of guidance "from heaven," are designed to help the people of Israel navigate their new life. (Ex 20:22) The guidance is grounded in the relationship that God has chosen to have with this people: "I am the Lord your God,"—which is another way of saying, "I am yours; and you are mine." The starting place is a relationship shaped by God's act of deliverance: "I am the Lord your God, who brought you out of the land of Egypt, out of the house of slavery." (Ex 20:2) What follows, in the 10 guiding words, is surely a recipe for them to enjoy their freedom, not any new form of enslavement. Living out the spirit of the guiding words will bring them a foretaste of what it means to realize God's reign among them.

The journey towards the promised land is far from plain sailing. It can even be seen as a huge 40-year detour. A detour, nevertheless, with glimpses of the glory of God and marked by provision of all the people's needs. While Moses himself will never enter the land of promise, his people's destination is clear. "Then Moses went up from the plains of Moab to Mount Nebo, … and the LORD showed him the whole land: … all the land of Judah as far as the Western Sea, the Negeb and the Plain … as far as Zoar." (Dt 34:1–4) They understood this to be the land promised to their forebears.

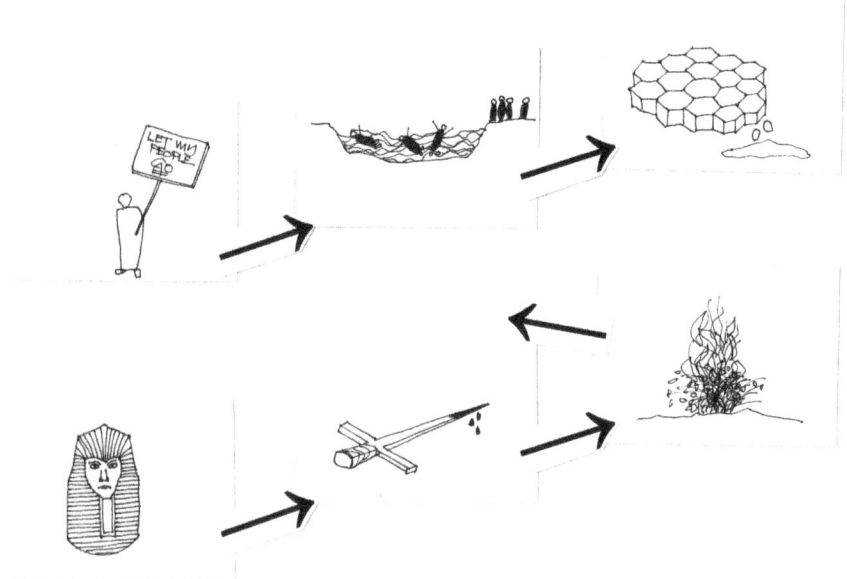

Image 1.13 Moses's Journey with Israel

Conclusion

Moses's infancy is marked by the challenge to address a child's basic needs for food, shelter and protection. As an adult, after the detour of killing an Egyptian taskmaster, Moses flees to the wilderness of Midian where he listens to God. He learns that God has noticed the suffering of the Israelites and has a plan for their deliverance in which Moses is pivotal. Returning to Egypt, and with his brother's help, Moses gains the ear of the Israelites. Despite repeated reversals, Moses maintains a demand for Pharaoh to let the Israelites go. Once a final plague results in the death of all the Egyptians' firstborn, Pharaoh and his people want the Israelites gone. Pharaoh later repents and sends his military might to retrieve them. Hemmed in, the Israelites escape through the sea on a dry path created by God. When Pharaoh's forces follow, the sea closes in and they are destroyed. Under Moses's leadership the Israelites then journey towards the land promised to their forebears, learning to enjoy a foretaste of God's reign.

Foundational Story 2: Jesus's Journey with Israel

The story of Jesus is the defining story of God and the foundational story for Christians. The gospel writers chart Jesus's journey with the people of Israel and those living alongside them in a land governed by the Roman Empire of their day. They depict Jesus as a second Moses, fulfilling the Mosaic calling. With Curle's framework in mind, we can again identify five key stages to the story, along with a couple of detours:

1 Infancy
  Detour: Flight to Egypt
2 Learning in Nazareth
  Detour: Driven into the Wilderness
3 Public Ministry: Confrontation
4 Crucifixion and Death
5 Resurrection

Let us briefly explore each one.

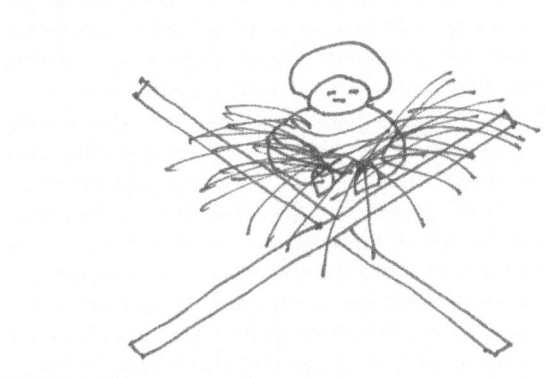

Image 1.14 Jesus's Infancy

Big Picture and Foundational Stories 35

Infancy

A Jewish couple, Joseph and Mary, are forced to travel from their home in Nazareth, to Bethlehem in the south of the country, to comply with the Roman Empire's census requirements. (Lk 2:1–5) While in Bethlehem, Mary gives birth to her firstborn, and "wrapped him in bands of cloth and laid him in a manger," because there was no place in the guest room. (Lk 2:6) The child is thus born far from the parental home, in temporary accommodation—in the city of the child's ancestor, David. Joseph names the child Jesus, the name given by an angelic messenger. (Mt 1:25, Lk 2:21) One striking aspect of Jesus's birth and early infancy is that it's a tale of the challenge to meet the child's basic needs, especially for shelter and protection, as faced by the infant Moses. The parental couple do the best they can to meet this child's needs, under testing circumstances.

Detour: Flight to Egypt

According to Matthew's account the child Jesus is threatened by the ruler of his day, just like the infant Moses. Herod fears a threat to his throne, after receiving intelligence from the *magi*, and searches for the child, "to destroy him." (Mt 2:13) Joseph is warned in a dream, and immediately "got up, took the child and his mother by night, and went to Egypt and remained there until the death of Herod." (Mt 2:14–15)

Image 1.15 Flight to Egypt

This can be viewed as a detour from the destiny that has been mapped out for Jesus to fulfil, of saving the Jewish people from their sins. Egypt is in the wrong direction. Ironically, it is a reversal of the detour taken by Moses, who fled Egypt for Midian. However, it is Joseph and Mary's best strategy for protecting Jesus from Herod's violent clutches. It also fulfils the prophet Hosea's ancient utterance, understood to apply to Jesus, that, "When Israel was a child, I loved him, and out of Egypt I called my son." (Hs 11:1)

Learning in Nazareth

The second stage of Jesus's life is his learning in Nazareth, where he spent much of his life.[37] Most of this is hidden from us. In the one surviving story of his adolescence, we find that Jesus learnt to understand and explore God's word revealed in the Hebrew Scriptures, to the amazement of many and the astonishment of his parents. (Lk 2:46–48) We assume that Jesus was apprenticed to Joseph's trade as a building contractor or craftsman, since he is later identified by the people of Nazareth as "the carpenter, the son of Mary." (Mk 6:3)

What is also clear, from his parables and teaching, is that Jesus learnt to understand his social setting, and acutely observed the social and relational dynamics of his locality. His parables reveal that he was alert to the social inequalities and injustices of his day.[38] For the best part of three decades he observed and noticed these. It meant that Jesus was deeply informed when he entered his public ministry, and his life and teaching spoke into these power dynamics.[39]

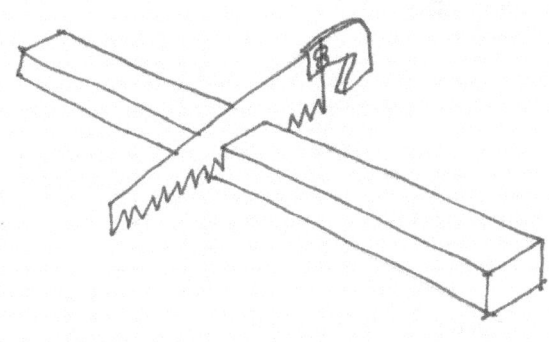

Image 1.16 Learning in Nazareth

Image 1.17 Driven into the Wilderness

Detour: Driven into the Wilderness

Jesus's public ministry is inaugurated at his baptism by John, in the Jordan river.[40] The gospels record a seismic event in which, as Jesus emerges from the water, the heavens are torn apart, the Spirit descends upon him like a dove, and a voice comes from heaven proclaiming, "You are my Son, the Beloved; with you I am well pleased." (Mk 1:11) It is a moment of supreme affirmation by God the Father.

However, rather than then moving straight into exercising a public ministry, the synoptics all have Jesus making an immediate detour into a solitary sojourn in the wilderness.[41] Jesus does not entirely go of his own choice, for it is "the Spirit [who] immediately drove him out into the wilderness." (Mk 1:12) There Jesus remains for a symbolic 40 days, living out an echo of the Israelites's 40-year nomadic journey before they entered the land of promise. However, it is an unconventional start to public ministry in any worldly sense. It is a significant time of testing and refining, alone apart from being "with the wild beasts, and the angels"—and confronted by the tempter, Satan. (Mk 1:13)

Doubtless, this is a vital time of preparation for all that Jesus will face over the following three years. However, it is a detour from what we might expect at the outset of a public ministry.

Image 1.18 Public Ministry: Confrontation

Public Ministry: Confrontation

On return from the wilderness, Jesus begins his public ministry up north, in Galilee, "after John was arrested." (Mk 1:14) He thus fills the prophetic space that John vacates. Jesus begins on the margins of Galilee, rather than moving straight to the center in Jerusalem. From the outset, what is striking is how much confrontation is involved as Jesus challenges the systems and diseases of his world.

Jesus begins by challenging everyone to change direction or "repent." (Mk 1:15) He then confronts "unclean" spirits. (Mk 1:23–27) Next, he heals those enduring debilitating sickness; and cleanses those outcast because of skin disease. (Mk 1:29–34, 40–45) He restores the paralyzed to walking, the withered to using their limbs again, and the deaf to hearing. (Mk 2:1–11, 3:1–5, 7:31–37) He stills the violent forces of nature. (Mk 4:35–41) He casts out a legion of demons from a tormented man; and restores a young girl from death. (Mk 5:1–13, 21–43) He challenges the rich to sell their possessions and give alms to the poor. (Mk 10:17–22) He gives sight back to the blind who have been reduced to beggary. (Mk 10:46–52) Then he disrupts the trade of those exploiting the poor in the temple precincts. (Mk 11:15–18)

These actions, and their frequent timing on the Jewish Sabbath, created huge hostility both from the intensely religious Jews, "Pharisees," and from leaders compromised with the Roman authorities, "Herodians." While often stridently opposed, these two parties came together and "conspired … against [Jesus], how to destroy him." (Mk 3:6) This was compounded by Jesus challenging the religious leaders' teaching about fasting, the Sabbath, care for one's parents, divorce, payment of Roman taxes, and showy religion. (Mk 2:18–28; 7:1–13; 10:1–12; 12:13–17, 38–40) Jesus's message and methods upset their understandings of what it meant to worship God faithfully.

It is not just the leaders. Jesus upsets his blood family, challenging the primacy of these societal bonds. (Mk 3:31–34)[42] This comes just after his family members have tried to restrain him because he had reportedly "lost his mind." (Mk 3:21) Jesus also challenges his disciples on several occasions, including when they argue about "who was the greatest." (Mk 9:33–37)

It is no surprise that Jesus is recorded as saying: "Do not think that I have come to bring peace to the earth; I have not come to bring peace, but a sword. For I have come to set a man against his father, and a daughter against her mother …." (Mt 10:34–39) Jesus was the great disruptor of his day. Many who met him—especially the religious and those in leadership—were disturbed and left feeling uncomfortable, angry, or defensive. Simultaneously, the spiritual forces of affliction and disease retreated and had their power broken by Jesus, who unshackled ordinary people from what oppressed them.

Image 1.19 Crucifixion and Death

Crucifixion and Death

The confrontation eventually climaxes in Jerusalem, the center of the Jewish world. Jerusalem, the city of peace, which "kills the prophets and stones those who are sent to it." (Lk 13:34–35) As Jesus repeatedly predicts to his disciples, it is "the chief priests, the scribes, and the elders"—leaders of his own people—who bring the confrontation to a head. (Mk 14:43) They hand him over to the Roman occupiers who govern the land; and then whip up a crowd to demand that Jesus be executed. After prevaricating and attempting to have Jesus released, the Roman governor Pilate accedes to their demand by issuing the order for Jesus to be crucified. (Mk 15:1–15)

Luke and Matthew point to the seismic nature of Jesus's death.[43] However, it is left to the apostle Paul and early church theologians to unpack this death's significance. Paul sees Jesus's death expiating the sin of humankind. (Rm 3:22–25) The writer to the Ephesians proclaims that Jesus's death has reconciled humanity to God and broken down the great dividing wall between Jew and Gentile, effecting a reconciliation that creates "one body through the cross." (Eph 2:11–20) The writer to the Colossian church puts it succinctly: "For in [Jesus] all the fullness of God was pleased to dwell, and through him God was pleased to reconcile to himself all things, whether on earth or in heaven, by making peace through the blood of his cross." (Col 1:19–20)

At the heart of these reflections is a clarity that Jesus's death has effected a fundamental change in the relationship which human beings have with God and with one another. Nothing will ever be the same again. Therefore, Paul boldly proclaims that, "if anyone is in Christ, there is a new creation." (2 Cor 5:17) The dynamics in the world have changed forever, and at the heart of this is an equality and unity among humanity before God. There is a systemic transformation of a supreme kind.

Resurrection

"If Christ has not been raised, your faith is futile," claims Paul. (1 Cor 15:17) As the apostle makes clear, Jesus's resurrection from the dead is the foundation of a Christian faith. (1 Cor 15:1–56) His resurrection offers hope to humanity that death will not have the last word. Rather, we will enjoy God's company for eternity, beyond the grave. However, this is not just "pie in the sky when you die." What Jesus's disciples down the ages have grasped, through the witness of Jesus's life and in recognizing the ongoing work of the Holy Spirit, is that we can experience a foretaste of heaven here on earth and realize more of God's reign among us.

After Jesus's resurrection, commenting on the healing of the crippled man at the temple gate, the apostle Peter proclaims that, "by faith in [Jesus's] name, his name itself has made this man strong, whom you see and know, and the faith that is through Jesus has given him this perfect health in the presence of all of you." (Acts 3:16) The wholeness and well-being that this healing evidenced is possible now: it is not just a future promise. This is important for understanding the signs, parables, and teaching of Jesus about "the kingdom of God," or "the kingdom of heaven."[44] This kingdom—God's realm—is breaking in now, as Jesus affirms: "For, in fact, the kingdom of God is among you." (Lk 17:21)

At the same time, as already noted, the present does not offer a full realization, only a foretaste of God's realm and the heavenly life that is to come. Jesus's resurrection provides the assurance that we are not just imagining this. It is a solid reality, just as his resurrected form was fully physical.[45] A reality whose outworking can be detected in the early Jerusalem church, when "the whole group of those who believed were of one heart and soul, and no one claimed private ownership of any possessions, but everything they owned was held in common." (Acts 4:32) The equality and unity among humanity effected by Christ's death and resurrection can be genuinely experienced on earth, even if only fleetingly.

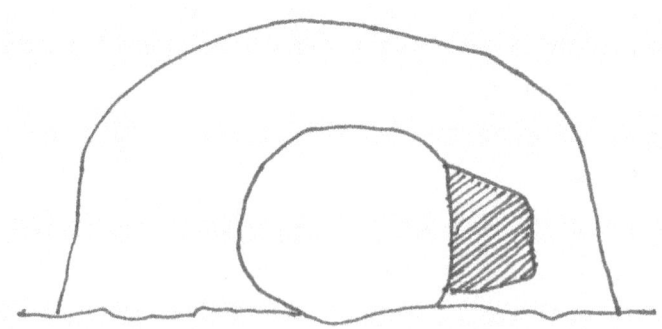

Image 1.20 Resurrection

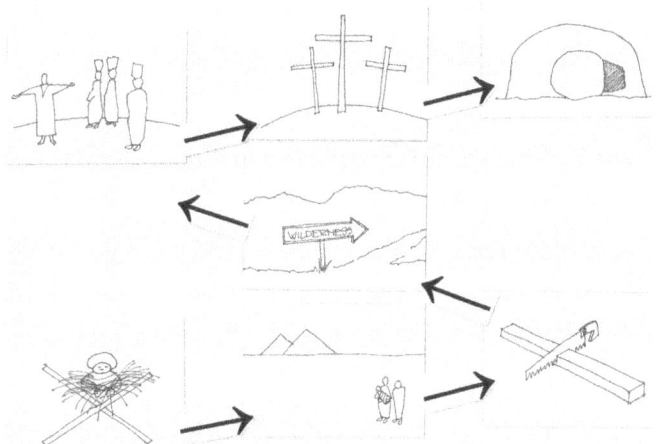

Image 1.21 Jesus's Journey with Israel

Conclusion

Jesus's infancy is marked by the challenge of addressing the child's basic needs for shelter and protection. The majority of Jesus's earthly life in Nazareth sees him learning to understand the culture and context within which he is living. Once Jesus moves into public ministry and offers a new way of living in the world, he comes into continual conflict with the Jewish leaders and religious people of his day. This culminates in Jesus's crucifixion. However, his death is not the defeat it seems. Instead, it fundamentally changes the world, opening the doorway to our reconciliation with God and to one another. Jesus's resurrection offers the hope both of a future heavenly banquet, and of experiencing a foretaste of that today.

Reconciling Mission

While it might seem artificial to superimpose Adam Curle's framework on these foundational Biblical narratives, doing so brings into focus the narrative arc. We notice that the overall flow of Curle's model is echoed in and extended by both stories. Or, we might say that Curle's model is rooted in a deep historical revelation of the way that God works in the world.

Both foundational narratives reveal that "detours" are crucial to the story. The detour may come about through human failure or violence, as with Moses's killing of the Egyptian taskmaster and Herod's threat to kill the infant Jesus, resulting in the "holy family" fleeing to Egypt and the massacre of innocent children in the Bethlehem locality. Or, the detour may arise through a driving of the Holy Spirit, as with Jesus's 40-day sojourn in the wilderness.

Moses's time in Midian proves vital in learning to listen to God, which will be key to his life's work, and in developing a strong family network. With Joseph and Mary, Jesus's early experience of being a migrant and then a refugee places God in identification with and thereby on the side of the migrant and marginalized of this world, those who are "disinherited."[46] Jesus's later adult baptism and testing in the wilderness proves his worthiness to fulfill all that God has in store for him, and provides a bedrock to his subsequent faithfulness, even unto death.

These illustrate how God integrates the detours in our lives within the fulfillment of our vocations when we are attentive to what God is doing and how God is calling. This is important to notice not just individually, but also for our corporate lives within local churches as we embark on "journeying out" and engaging more deeply with our neighbors and local communities.[47]

Curle's model highlights that both foundational Biblical narratives have important lessons to teach us about the dynamics of power and conflict. Hence, our need to attend to such dynamics as we seek to join in with God's great mission. A mission that is encapsulated by the writer to the Colossians proclaiming that in and through Jesus, "God was pleased to reconcile to himself all things, whether on earth or in heaven, by making peace through the blood of his cross." (Col 1:19–20) As revealed in Jesus, God's mission is a reconciling one, to reconcile *all things* to God's self.

What Curle's model and these Biblical narratives highlight is that such reconciliation involves a practical outworking in which social injustice and inequality are redressed. There is no reconciliation without a restoration of true justice and equity in human relationships. As we seek to participate in God's reconciling mission, in our local contexts, we can therefore usefully check ourselves against the flow of these narratives, informed by Curle's framework.

Questions for Reflection and Group Discussion

1 What did you find most striking about the theoretical framework offered in this chapter? How does it connect with or disrupt your existing thinking about a local church's missional engagement with her locality?

2 What did you find most stimulating about the presentation of the foundational Biblical stories offered here, and why? What other Biblical narratives do you see resonating with this offering, either in a complementary way, or in tension with it?

3 What does this chapter prompt you to want to reconsider or revisit in your reading and understanding of the Biblical witness, and why?

2 Applying *Reconciling Mission* Insights in England

An Initial Story: Crafty Café in Berkswich Parish

To mark the centenary of the end of World War I in 2018, the parish church of Berkswich had experimented with inviting local schools to create poppies to form an artwork installation that flowed through their church building. This creative activity emerged through a conversation with the local branch of the Royal British Legion and a Scouts group, and first raised an awareness among Graham and Vicki Adamson, the vicar and his wife, that there was an interest in artistic creativity in their local community.

During Advent 2020, when Covid-19 restrictions still applied, Graham Adamson invited anyone in the community to pick a Christmas carol and decorate a window in their home with the carol's story. Some put out statues in their front garden. Others used tissue paper and made a stained-glass window. Astonishingly, 200 households in the parish responded creatively to the idea. The Adamsons shared an online map so that residents knew where to visit the array of windows. This included an invitation to donate to the local hospice, whose fundraising had been hit during the pandemic. Key was releasing local people to use their imagination and trusting that they would engage respectfully. This unearthed unexpected treasure and wide participation in the community.

On the first anniversary of the initial Covid-19 lockdown, in March 2021, the Adamsons wanted to offer a way for local people to respond to the losses they had faced. They invited people to draw, paint, or stitch a message on pieces of fabric, to form a type of bunting or collection of prayer flags. However, "We deliberately didn't call them prayer flags," to avoid creating a stumbling block. The flags were then hung from the lychgate—the boundary between the street and the entrance to the church grounds and graveyard. The Adamsons set no limits. "We took a risk on people. They could've written, 'F U Covid' on the flags." Again, many local people responded creatively and appropriately.

Vicki Adamson had been doing formal study in textiles art and was required to fulfill a brief to make a centerpiece for an exhibition. Mindful also that there was no obvious "bumping space" for artists, she said to her husband: "Why don't we actually mount an art exhibition?"[1] With support from the lay leaders, they opened up the church building for an art exhibition by local people, especially seeking those who had started creating during the pandemic. People brought in their work and talked about what had elicited their artistic endeavors. For example, a mother and three daughters were all living separately. None had painted before. During lockdown, they watched the same online tutorials, and each made a painting in response. It brought them joy. Unsure of their skill level, they wondered how others would respond. Sharing their paintings through the exhibition, and telling their story, brought delight from hearing others remark, "That's so great. Why don't I try something like that?" The exhibition offered a place for hidden treasure in the neighborhood to be unearthed, shared and celebrated—and act as inspiration for others.

The Adamsons emphasized that they did not impose any censorship. The church took the risk of leaving local people to decide for themselves what would be suitable to offer, with a wide diversity of artwork exhibited, everything from conventional paintings to crocheted toilet roll covers.

Prompted by participation in the *Reconciling Mission* program, the Adamsons saw the need to keep working at addressing people's mental health while building on local interest in artistic creativity. This led to the establishment of Crafty Café, a weekly gathering in the church building where people could come and try out a craft activity. The aim was to have an intentionally supportive environment ("We didn't want it to be a stitch-and-bitch!"), where anyone could come and feel comfortable, including those with mental health challenges and neuro-diverse people. Craft activities at different tables are led by people from the local community and by church members. Central is offering a space for people to share their stories. For example, one older man, whose wife had died during the pandemic, brought in her unfinished tapestries. A lady from outside the church taught him how to do the needlepoint, and he worked initially to finish the tapestry of a deer, while sharing stories about his wife and his pain at losing her. Treasure was found within the group, and a safe space for processing grief.

Mary Sapsford, one of the lay leaders of Crafty Café, shared what a blessing it has become.

> I look at Crafty Café, hear the buzz, and see so much caring and love going on. I think of one very quiet lady who joined us a year ago, when grieving for her partner who'd just died. Now, she comes early. If she sees somebody sitting on their own, she'll go and sit by them to see if they'd like to be in conversation. It's beautiful. It's unlocked kindness and treasure that was hidden away in our community. It just fills me with joy.[2]

Description

The *Reconciling Mission* program was developed as an offering by Reconciliation Initiatives, a not-for-profit organization based in England.[3] It is an 18-month learning and development program for clergy, sponsored in small groups of four to six participants. Up until 2025, these groups all came from an Anglican diocese in England, Wales, or Scotland, sponsored by their bishop and senior staff. Up to half a dozen diocesan groups form a cohort who engage with the program together. Cohorts began in 2020, 2021, and 2022, with participants from 16 dioceses from across the Church of England, the Church in Wales and the Scottish Episcopal Church. A fourth cohort, with four diocesan groups, began in 2024, and a fifth cohort formed of three diocesan groups began in 2025. Future groups are expected to be drawn from different denominational backgrounds not just Anglican, beginning with a sixth cohort in 2026.

The program begins with a residential learning week, which is key to building relationships across the cohort. It also provides a container for dynamically exploring content: various frameworks, approaches, tools, and ways of thinking. These include: the theoretical and theological frameworks covered in Chapter 1; an introduction to "dwelling in the word"; a geographical mapping process; a range of processes, ways of thinking and community-building ideas inspired by an Asset-Based Community Development (ABCD) approach; and an introduction to a group coaching process drawing on an action learning set model.[4] ABCD is a developed methodology that builds on the gifts, knowledge, passions, and experience of the people living in a neighborhood.[5] In a British context, ABCD has been given a theological articulation by Al Barrett and Ruth Harley. Their approach is drawn on within the *Reconciling Mission* program, in which Barrett and one of his local colleagues are key resource contributors.[6]

After the initial residential, the program offers an online group coaching process for participants, over 18 months, to support them in implementing their learning and in sharing it with local lay leaders and clergy colleagues.[7] There are two further in-person gatherings, usually at Coventry Cathedral: a day conference midway through, and another at the conclusion of the program: these provide an opportunity to offer further inspiration, to share stories and insights together, and to reconnect as a group in person.[8]

The first three program cohorts were independently evaluated by Dr Joanna Sadgrove, and the summaries of her main findings have been published.[9] Among the benefits of the program highlighted by Sadgrove are:

- The strength of peer support and noncompetitive collegiality in the process of addressing missional challenges.
- The value of connection with fundamental questions about mission, ministry, and sharing good news; and an articulation of the value of working in partnership with local people and organizations.
- The importance of prioritizing the work of listening, to peers, congregation members, local people, and the Holy Spirit, to discern how God is at work.
- The evolutionary journey and development of existing and new forms of outreach to local neighborhoods in collaboration with a wide range of organizations beyond the church.

Illustrative Stories and Key Features

There are potentially three movements needed within a local church to become more missional and aligned to God's reconciling mission, as this author sees it:

1 A first movement is *reorienting to be outward-looking and outward-facing*, moving beyond being—at its very simplest—a social club that gathers to sing God's praises and break bread together.[10]

2 A second movement is the shift from the church as a provider of services to address need, to the church as a *partner with others and recipient of their gifts*.

3 A third movement sees a *shift to the church as guest*, dependent on or receiving from others, whilst appropriately playing her own part.

The third movement is a reversal from being the host, where the church expects others to come to us on our terms, which has tended to characterize so much of the church's outreach in Western societies.[11] Reading the gospels, it is striking how integral to Jesus's public ministry was his experience of being the guest, not the host, and of meeting others in situations where they had the upper hand as hosts.

What follows are stories and examples drawn from interviews with a small selection of participants in the second cohort of the *Reconciling Mission* program.[12] These seek to draw out some of the features of the contextual missional approach encouraged by the program.

Shifting the Thinking about Local Community

How a church thinks about its local community is significant. During their time in the parish of Berkswich, Graham and Vicki Adamson have contributed to a shift that has happened in their church's thinking about their neighbors. Graham began the story:

> *During my first couple of years here, and beforehand, the congregation was trying to pay off a debt to the diocese. They had a regular routine, with a diarized package of social activities, all focused on fundraising. These were old-fashioned and dated activities, which were not good at including people outside the church. When the pandemic first hit, all that stopped. Since then, we've come back with some events with a fundraising dimension. For example, we've started holding a regular makers' market, for arts and crafts people to show their wares. We charge the stall holders for their stalls. But it feels very different. Our main aim is not to make money: that's not the primary purpose. Before, the question was, "What can the church gain from such an event?" Now, the question is: "How can we provide a platform for people to share what they have to offer?" Thus, a big step with our Christmas fair was to bring the event into the main church building, not just in the church hall. It was a sign that we were valuing what people had to offer.*

Vicki Adamson picked up the thread:

Importantly, we talk with people at the stalls. They might not actually buy anything, but we've had a conversation: we've started to build a relationship. That's a sign of a shift in how we view our neighbors. Before it was, "Oh, they're a source of income to help us pay off the church debt." Now we see our neighbors as people we want to get to know and be in relationship with.

Their lay colleague Mary Sapsford continued:

Another thing we've now done with our Christmas fair is to invite other charities to come in and have a stall. So, it's not just about the church. They come in, have their own stall, and promote their own organization. Some in the congregation frowned on this initially. But now it's embraced as a sign of valuing what others are contributing to our community.

Vicki Adamson then made this striking observation:

When Graham applied for the job, one of the phrases that stuck in my head was that the parish said they wanted a vicar who would change the narrative in the community about the church. But I'd say the biggest change has been to the narrative told in the church about the community. The main refrain is no longer that we need to bring them in here, or that they need to come to us. Now there's a focus on how we're engaging as part of the wider community. This means we're asking, "Who and what are we connecting into?" It's shown in apparently small things, such as the choir going to sing Christmas carols at the community Christmas event or at a local old people's home. The main concern is no longer: "We need to get more members into our choir." Rather people are asking, "What can we contribute this time? What will we sing to bless others?" The narrative has changed. The focus has swapped, and been turned on its head.

Mary Sapsford encapsulated the shift that has occurred: "We're no longer inward-thinking. Our parish hashtag, of being 'God's Loving Community,' wasn't one that we were really doing before. Now we're doing better at actually living that out. The story has been turned on its head." This is a classic example of a shift from being an inward-looking church into one that is outward-facing. Berkswich parish church is now exploring how they can contribute to their neighborhood, rather than being focused on what their neighbors can give to the church, or whether they are coming to their church services.

Sometimes a structural change can contribute to such a shift. In the parish of St Anne's, Chasetown, the vicar, Richard Westwood, introduced a striking innovation to the church's regular worship pattern. Once a month the church now holds a "community service." This is the main Sunday worship service, built around a particular theme and incorporating a visiting speaker from the local community. Speakers have come from a wide range of sources, including from local schools, the local football club, or one of the church's community engagement projects. Westwood articulated the rationale: "The idea is to try and make sure that those within the gathered Sunday congregation get to hear and have their eyes opened to what's going on around them. The community service drip feeds this, on a month-by-month basis. We're asking: 'Have you noticed that *this* is happening in your community?'"

These community services are a striking example of a culture-shaping step: incorporating a window into diverse community activities within a church's worshipping life helps to break down the sacred and secular divide. They serve to affirm that God is interested in all of life.

Graham Adamson named an important element of a church's attitudinal shift as having the grace and courage to receive the gifts of others in the local neighborhood, instead of seeing herself as needing to be the provider of services to their neighbors. He illustrated this:

> *Shortly after starting on the* Reconciling Mission *program, I discovered that there was a local group that runs repair cafés. A repair café is where they have tables of experts available to fix someone's broken down vacuum cleaner, toaster, gardening equipment, or whatever; or to mend a torn garment. However, the local group didn't always have a suitable venue. So, I offered them our church building as a space for them to host one of their repair cafés. They did all the advertising and brought in all the experts. It was hugely popular. The church was filled with people coming to get things repaired. The energy all came from outside the church, and we simply supported their endeavors by providing a space. However, I wouldn't have risked doing that without the* Reconciling Mission *program encouraging me to have the confidence that people would respect our church space.*

Becoming a Guest

Perhaps a deeper shift occurs when the church moves from a hosting role into that of being a guest. Luci Morriss is a rural pioneer priest with responsibility for the Borderlink Benefice, a group of parishes in the Diocese of Hereford, probably the most rural diocese in the Church of England. Morriss and one of her lay leaders, Ange Grunsell, reflected on the significance of their church getting involved the previous year in Hay Pride. This was the first gay pride festival in Hay-on-Wye, the nearest big town to their small parishes. Grunsell began:

Participating in Hay Pride was an interesting opportunity for our church to affirm something positive about our attitude. That first year, we had a stall and set aside the time to be involved all day. It was striking how many people came up and said, "It's brilliant to see the church here." People of a huge range of ages, including young people, coming up and saying this as well as people from other churches in the area. It was inspirational and enabled a whole host of conversations. It also affirmed for people that the church can have positive things to say about people's sexuality.

Luci Morriss picked up the baton:

When we first approached the organizers, we went with trepidation, given the negative reputation of the wider church in relation to same-sex relationships. Hay Pride was a local community initiative, and the organizers were surprised but pleased when we said that, as a church, we'd really like to be part of the festival. We were also prepared for some resistance from within our congregations; and for a potentially hostile response from some people in the community in how they might receive our participation. So, we prepared ourselves for how to respond without being defensive. But, as it turned out, it couldn't have been more positive. We had some powerful conversations about why some of us in the church felt it was important to be present there. I think that created a shift in people's attitudes to us as a church. It has led on to better and stronger conversations in the intervening months before this year's festival. So, I'm hoping that this can become a regular commitment to participate as a church. Because participating in Hay Pride expresses something of our commitment to work for justice and change in the world; and calling that out. I found it incredibly moving that there was a real sense, both times we've been part of the festival procession, from such different parts of our community and beyond, of all these people having an incredible feeling of oneness in our desire to see positive change.

The shift that is being identified here is one that Luci Morriss named as an insight from her participation in the *Reconciling Mission* program:

I continue to wrestle with those questions, "Who's the host? And, who's the guest?"

We're moving away from a model where the church was always the host and invited other people in, and "they" were made welcome – although often only up to a degree, until they tried to make changes. Now we're moving to doing more joining in with other's initiatives and activities, and having to face the question, "How does it feel for us to be the guest in the wider community?"

Morriss identifies a potential discomfort for the church. Such discomfort accompanies a shift in the balance of power resulting from being the guest instead of the host. As the guest, one has less control over what happens and how, and must be willing to accommodate others' preferences and approach and work out how the church can join in.

Exploring Uncomfortable Ground and Asking Deeper Questions

Engaging with something which may feel uncomfortable has the potential to be fruitful, as Esther Allen, a lay leader at St Anne's, Chasetown, realized in her parish:

During the height of the Covid pandemic, we noticed that men were less likely to pick up the phone and reach out to others. Men's mental health can be an uncomfortable subject. But, here at St Anne's, we think it's good to explore uncomfortable areas. The issue crystallized when a local man with mental health issues, whom we knew, disappeared. In responding to this, someone had the idea that men might warm to going on a walk together and being able to talk while they walked. There wasn't anything similar locally that I'd come across. But we could see the potential therapeutic benefits. So, we launched a 'Men's Wellbeing Walk' on Monday mornings, to help address male mental health; but under the umbrella of Burntwood Be A Friend, rather than as a church project. There's easy access and no pressure to share, just the opportunity to walk – and to talk if desired. The group is a mixture of guys of all ages in the community and St Anne's congregation members, that walk together every week. They provide one another with mutual peer support. One chap who comes regularly, and who's a long-term carer for a wife with significant physical health issues, says it's been an absolute lifeline. Others have made similar comments. This project has led to a partnership with the local health authority, who now refer people to us; and to linking up with MIND, a mental health charity, who offer drop-in sessions for additional support.

It is notable how a public body, the local health authority, recognized the value of this small initiative developed by a local church; and how the church was also able to link up with a specialist mental health organization to provide greater structured support where that might be needed. The vicar of the parish, Richard Westwood, told the story of how the larger community project had developed:

Burntwood Be A Friend started amidst the pandemic. As soon as the first lockdown happened in March 2020, myself, Esther Allen, another church leader, and a local elected councilor, all said, "We can't do nothing here." We tried to set up something quickly which would enable food to be provided for those in need. It included a helpline for those who wanted advice, medical prescription deliveries for those isolating, and so forth. As the pandemic played through, we became aware of levels of need – emotional and mental health needs but also levels of poverty – that had been hidden beforehand.

There was then a key moment in the summer of 2021, just after I began on the Reconciling Mission *program, when those of us involved needed to decide: does this come to an end now that the pandemic's seemingly over? Or can we morph Burntwood Be A Friend into becoming something good that has longer legs than just a Covid mutual-aid group? The program helped me to be clear that there was a legitimate role for the church in helping to shape this. The existing partnerships that our church had with Spark, a local project to help give young children a good start in life, and our collaboration with other churches and the borough council, helped us to press the 'go' button, and to justify the time and energy of my own involvement.*

Whilst St Anne's is the registered base for Burntwood Be A Friend, we've now got a separate community store, as it outgrew the space available in our hall. While the church was initially able to offer physical space, the fact that it's now moved out of St Anne's is a healthy thing. We've not tried to retain ownership. Instead, we've asked, "Who else is going to be involved?" The number of volunteers now contributing to running Burntwood Be A Friend is way beyond anything the church could have done alone. It indicates how welcoming and inviting it's been for those people. Sure, we've faced our challenges. But, through the program, I discovered the surefootedness for us to evolve in a turbulent time. And it has given me confidence to try and sniff out places where there might be something for the church to collaborate in, along with others; or to champion a cause that's happening, which we might not have any direct input into.

Westwood went on to reflect upon the impact of St Anne's participation in this community project, and the deeper questions that the church faced as a result:

The church's involvement in Burntwood Be A Friend prompted us to ask deeper questions: "Why's it like this? How come we didn't know there were people in our community who don't have enough food for their children? Why is that the situation? And how do we address the wake-up call needed in local people's minds?" There's now a greater level of awareness, both within the church fellowship and in the wider community groups we're linked to, that it's not enough to say, "Here's some food." Or, "You're going through a difficult time, let me put my arm around you," metaphorically. The question also has to be, "Why is it like this?"

However, this can lead us to take a stand on things, which can be uncomfortable or risk upsetting local officials, some of whom we're trying to work collaboratively with. So, there was a young homeless man who ended up staying with us in the vicarage. I had to make repeated calls to the borough council's housing department and have arguments with officials to try and get him housed. There was also some alarm for people in the church. They'd heard about homelessness and knew of it as a concept. But when you have someone who arrives at church saying, "I was sleeping in Lichfield under the carpark ramp last night," then it suddenly brings the reality home. Which then awakens the important "Why?" question. Unless you get near to the issues, you don't feel the need to ask the question. If you stay back from the mess as a church, or as a human, then you're not going to feel the need to say, "What's wrong here?" Because you may think that wrong things are only happening elsewhere. There's a journey now for our church to see the wider issues of society as being a challenge for all of us.

An emphasis on the church as collaborative partner, rather than being the primary provider, was a theme that recurred throughout the interview with Westwood. He made this observation:

> *We're a small local church; we're not a megachurch. So, even if we wanted to, we couldn't be the source of all good things that happen in this community. To make a contribution, we've had to take on a role of collaborator. This means saying we want to support and encourage things that we think are good, that others are doing. Even though it's not under our umbrella.*

When asked for an illustration, Westwood responded with this story:

> *We were approached 18 months ago by a local Scout group saying that one of their members, George, was going to the World Scout Jamboree in Korea, and could he give a presentation at our church to raise some funds.[13] On the face of it there was no particular benefit to St Anne's. But, I said, "Of course. Yes, please come." We incorporated George and some of his fellow Scouts into our monthly community worship service. They came and told us about their planned trip to Korea. Since that first visit, George has returned five or six times, to give an update. The church has adopted him in some ways. But then, remarkably, George said, "We'd like to come and help you. Please can we have a stall at your Christmas fair? And can we help you with organizing and setting up the fair?" I don't know where it's going to end. It hasn't yet. But I know that George and his group feel St Anne's is their church, and that we've put rocket boosters on their participation in the World Scout Jamboree. In the process, there's been a mutual flourishing, for him and for St Anne's. His parents – who aren't churchgoers – feel that this has been a good place for George to grow. He's now involved in local politics, as a Youth Councilor, and has been vocal about injustice and local issues. We've seen him thrive and grow in confidence. It's been fantastic to observe, and we've helped to encourage him.*

Mutual Flourishing and Humbly Receiving

This sense of mutual flourishing and benefit that can come from engaging openly with local people and organizations was also expressed by Vicki Adamson and Mary Sapsford as they reflected on Crafty Café, described in the opening story of this chapter and hosted by their church. Adamson expressed it this way:

> *People in the local community are giving to each other – and to us as well. My mum has Alzheimer's disease and suffers with dementia. I've found it challenging and not known how to deal with it. But there are people at Crafty Café who've got much more experience with dementia. They've given me ways of understanding what's going on with my mother that have made it easier for me to cope with. That's been so valuable to me.*

Such mutuality was affirmed by Mary Sapsford, who noted:

> *I remember sitting down at Crafty Café one day. I'd had a difficult week and expressed this out loud – but then thought perhaps I shouldn't have said anything because I'm supposed to be helping to lead the gathering. However, the group picked up on my struggle and took off with it: they talked about women and what was expected of women in society. It became a wonderful, deep conversation, which I get a lot out of. All just prompted by me being vulnerable with the group.*

Reflecting on this aspect of Crafty Café, Vicki Adamson expressed a shift that may be required for those coming from some church traditions:

> *It was important to us that this wasn't going to be the church offering this service to you, and you're going to gratefully receive it. Rather, we're creating a space and a community, knowing that means us receiving humbly as well. Which can be hard if you come from a tradition that says the church has all the answers. For us, it's been important to recognize instead that we don't have all the answers, and that this can be a communal growing for all involved.*

Cultural Shift and Polarity Management

Luci Morriss identified a different change in thinking and culture that can contribute to a more missionally-minded church. Morriss spoke of a sense that the church cannot act on her own, but instead needs to be attentive to her neighbors, notice what is emerging and bubbling up, and look at how to affirm those developments, and join in with or support them in some way. This might include making a financial contribution from the church to a community initiative, rather than the church expecting the money to flow the other way. Morriss added:

> *There's also something needed in terms of letting go. Some of our church members need to see that there are people within the congregation who want to be released to do different things and engage with others outside the church. The temptation is for them to be thinking, "Oh, this is a younger, able person and therefore we could get them to do this or that job in the church." Whereas maybe what God wants for that person is, yes, they might worship with us to be filled; but then their more important role might be engaging with another group entirely in the community. That's a real cultural shift, isn't it?*

The cultural shift that Morriss identifies is from a church which sees herself as central and therefore having first call on people's time and commitments, to being alongside in a supportive role that resources people for engagement in other groups or organizations that are blessing the local community. For Morriss, this connected to the need for a wider shift in thinking: "We have quite a fight on our hands. The national church doesn't help with their attention on, 'How do we fund our priests?', which is driven so much more by a sense of scarcity than one of abundance. Trying to get people to trust that God's in this with us, is quite a struggle, isn't it?" Morriss further expanded on this:

> *With the rise of the internet, place and time have ceased to be so significant for younger people. The sense of the village as the place where things happen has been eroded over a long time. But for older people it remains. And the church is probably one of the last expressions of that, with a sense that, "We're really going to fight for this! Because the shops have gone. The pub's gone. The school's closed. We haven't had our own vicar for 40 years – but we're still going to struggle on."*
>
> *However, I fear that if we keep giving our best energy to the chaplaincy model of the existing congregation, rather than the more radical role of being-out-in-the-community, by the time we've finished our role as chaplains, we'll turn around and our opportunity will have gone. In a time of polarization, we need to be both-and, don't we? Holding that tension, both lay people and clergy, of avoiding over-exerting ourselves, but trying to live in a healthy kingdom-like way, as we try and be both pastoral chaplains and missional engagers in the community.*

Morriss here identifies a classic polarity which needs to be managed, rather than a problem to be solved: how to balance ministry, or "pastoral chaplaincy," with missional engagement in the local neighborhood. Both are needed for a healthy church. Even if the balance in many churches needs to be tilted more towards missional engagement than has been the case in recent years.

The Purpose of the Church

The above type of shift can lead us into asking some fundamental questions about the purpose of the church, which Richard Westwood and the parish of St Anne's have wrestled with:

> *One thing we've asked with more honesty is, "What's the purpose of the church? Is it simply to have regular worship which is well attended?" Which the inherited model of church would say, "This is foundationally what we're here for, to make Christian disciples; and the way that we'll see that evidenced is if folks come regularly on a Sunday." Whereas I think the bigger question is, "What does God want of God's church?"—which gets answered in a wider, more nuanced way. How we fill the pews becomes less important when we're aware of God's dream for God's world. Given that the Church of England has thousands of inherited buildings, rarely fit for purpose, and which may not be what's needed for God's kingdom purposes now—there are difficult questions to be asked about that.*
>
> *How this lands for St Anne's is important. Because the church was built by a benefactor, the owner of the local mines, for his workers so that they had somewhere to worship on a Sunday. Today, however, St Anne's has had to reinvent its own sense of purpose. If we're just looking to have local workers come here on a Sunday, that's not enough. St Anne's sense of itself now, portrayed in the vision statement we've agreed, is about an open-hearted and open-handed generosity in seeing God's kingdom thrive locally. Seeking the fingerprints of God's kingdom in all that we do, with openness and inclusivity. With a generosity that says, "These are the hallmarks of God's kingdom, wherever it happens."*
>
> *Clearly, we'd like more people coming to worship—but that's not the measure of our success. People in the church now say, "What have we been a catalyst for? What questions have we provoked in people's minds by the way we've gone about our lives? In the way that we've lived hopefully, generously, and sacrificially for the benefit of our community." And if we provoke such questions, as Jesus did for the Pharisees who asked, "Why are you doing this?" then that's a healthy journey to be on.*

What might it look like for our churches to reflect more deeply on "God's dream for God's world"? This suggests giving deeper attention to releasing more of the kingdom of heaven here on earth. Within this, Westwood here identifies a distinctive calling for the local church to live hopefully, generously, and sacrificially for the benefit of her local community. When a local church does so, Westwood is confident that living in such a way will prompt people to ask *why*. This can then begin a conversation which leads others on a path to exploring following Jesus for themselves.

Shifting from Church to God Questions and Amplifying Community Flourishing

Richard Westwood went on to ponder his potential legacy: "Whoever follows me as minister, I would hope that the future leadership approach will be open-eyed and outward-facing. Which will mean not being so anxious about, 'How do we keep the doors open?' but rather asking, 'How do we go out through those doors and be a part of whatever God's doing in our community?'" Here Westwood articulates an insight shared through the *Reconciling Mission* program: the importance of shifting from asking church questions, to asking God questions. Classic church questions revolve around how to fill the empty seats, how the finances will be raised to keep ministry continuing, and how aging buildings can be maintained. These questions tend to be driven by anxiety and a sense of scarcity, at least in the context of declining church attendance that typifies significant portions of the Church of England and other mainline denominations in the UK. These church questions can consume most of the time and attention of those involved in church leadership and governance.

In contrast, God questions seek to explore what God is doing within a particular neighborhood, or among a particular segment of the local population. Such questions assume that the Holy Spirit is active throughout the world, including among our neighbors, and that the church can discern such activity if she opens her eyes and pays attention. God questions are inspired by curiosity and a sense of the abundance that flows from God. They can be energizing for the local church, releasing church members from the burdens of church questions, and giving a sense of hopefulness in the process of discerning where God is at work in their neighborhood.

Exploring God questions is facilitated by building on church members' connections within a locality. Commenting on St Anne's, Chasetown, Esther Allen noted that: "In terms of our connections with others beyond the church, those happen in so many different ways: it's closely interwoven, that flow. If you tried to map it out, it would almost be impossible because there'd be so many squiggly lines going all over the place." This was affirmed by Richard Westwood, who added:

> *It's almost viral, isn't it? It's something to be cherished because there's an organic process which we couldn't design ourselves. Which, for me, suggests that God's at work. We're recognizing that there are people who we haven't yet met who are already doing the sorts of things where we'd want to say, "God loves this: let's help it thrive." People come forward with ideas, and part of our approach must be to try and find a way to say, "Yes," if we can – if it's going to be something which will enable the local community to thrive.*

Westwood's approach to exploring God questions embodies what is at the heart of this apparently simple idea. He's encouraging the parish of St Anne's to ask: "In what ways is what others are doing something which God loves? And how can we in the church help those good things to thrive?" This places the church alongside her neighbors, seeking to work with and to support or amplify what is enabling their local community to flourish.

Being Small and Accepting Having Enough

At the conclusion of his interview, Graham Adamson, of Berkswich parish, identified a significant learning for him from the *Reconciling Mission* program:

> *We're in a relatively affluent area but we're not a rich church. We're an older, smaller congregation, without much technological know-how. So, we're not well-resourced. But we've been able to engage missionally with our neighbors. If we can, anyone can. It doesn't need the whizz-bang resources. It just needs people to be willing to love, to take risks, to dig for those treasures, and to work with what's there among the people in the community. We've spoken a lot about crafts and the art scene, because that's where the treasure's emerged here. Connecting those up with addressing people's mental health and neurodiversity challenges in our locality seems to have become our calling. It could well be different in other places. But every parish in this country has resources*

that they can dig for, to help address the issues in their context. It doesn't need big finances. It doesn't need complicated programs. We don't even have proper kitchen facilities in our church building for making tea and coffee. But we make it work. We didn't even have tables, but someone found some online. We've got enough. It'd be nice to have other stuff, but we have enough.

Adamson identifies a core conviction of the *Reconciling Mission* program, that being a small church is not a hindrance to missional engagement because there are treasures to be unearthed in every community. There are people and organizations motivated to address their local challenges and to contribute to the flourishing of their neighborhood. Adamson also names an important theological principle: that God will provide the church with enough for what she is called to contribute within her context—their "daily bread."

Reintegrating Detours

In each of the case studies, the churches had faced "detours" of different kinds. Richard Westwood offered this illustration from the parish of St Anne's:

In 2017 our church council received a small grant from Lichfield Diocese to take forward our plans for an after-school youth club. Equipment was bought and a partnership was set up with a Christian organization, Youth for Christ (YFC). YFC provided a trained worker to lead volunteers in running an after-school club for young people aged 8 to 13 years old. The gathering was called Tuesday Hub, and the group got off to a good start with encouraging numbers participating and positive engagement by the youth. However, after the original YFC worker moved on in 2019, things did not work out well with their replacement: volunteers lost their confidence and the Tuesday Hub gathering struggled. Then the new worker also left. I was left "holding the baby," along with a skeleton group of hesitant volunteers. The Covid-19 pandemic proved the death knell. We just didn't have the energy to restart Tuesday Hub as we emerged out of the pandemic restrictions.

In 2020, it seemed like our church's idea for reaching local young people had died. However, after an extended hiatus, in the spring of 2024 our parish was approached by the leaders of FunClub, an established local youth club. Their purpose-built club premises had been sold against FunClub's wishes: the building was then demolished to make space for a much-needed new health center. But the promised new premises for FunClub never materialized. They were now homeless. So, FunClub asked us if they could use St Anne's once a month for an evening youth club.

There were risks for us. FunClub has many more and older youth members, with a wider range of challenging needs than Tuesday Hub had ever catered for. However, the church council decided it was a risk worth taking. We agreed a six-month trial. When this went well, the church council agreed to the arrangement continuing into 2025. Our church offers a small team of volunteers who attend FunClub and help to host and welcome the young people and the FunClub staff.

Amazingly, on the back of this strengthening partnership, a local business with a heart for our community recently agreed to fund all the costs of FunClub being run at St Anne's for 12 months: staff salaries, session costs, all the heating and hosting involved for St Anne's – the lot! The business went even further, offering to fund some of St Anne's other work with children and families in 2025. God knew our heart for serving young people in our community. Through working in partnership with others, we're now able to contribute to the flourishing of local young people in ways we'd never imagined before the pandemic. God has done more than we ever imagined.

Westwood's account illustrates a pattern where something which is experimented with in the church can fall flat or seem to "fail" in some way; but the desire to serve can be reborn in unexpected and more fruitful ways when a church engages in a deeper partnership with others in the local community. God is able to redeem and reincorporate into a parish's story something that previously looked like a painful detour.

Centrality of Relationship-Building

Central to much of what was shared through the interviews was the importance of relationship-building with neighbors and exploring ways to work in some level of partnership. Such partnerships can take on a number of different forms:

1. Listening to what others in the locality are passionate about, or care about, or are organized for, such as the gay pride event that the Borderlink Benefice joined in with;
2. Opening the church space up to be used by others for their purpose, such as hosting a community-run repair café in Berkswich parish church, or a youth club in St Anne's parish;

3   Sharing the church space with other groups, as with Berkswich parish church's Christmas fair, so other local groups can publicize what they offer;

4   Building relationships with people in need, as Richard Westwood and St Anne's parish did with a homeless person; and then exploring why they are facing such injustice;

5   Building relationships through an activity offered by the church, such as Crafty Café in Berkswich parish church, which can lead to mutually supportive pastoral conversations; and,

6   Paying for a service, such as outward-bound leadership for youth in the Borderlink Benefice, which Luci Morriss spoke of in her interview, and which then led to developing a strong relationship with one of the staff who subsequently offered to provide voluntary leadership for outward-bound opportunities for local youth.

Richard Westwood offered one of the keys to genuine relationship-building and partnership: "Provided we can spot the possibilities, and not seek to dominate, but look to collaborate, that then slowly builds up a level of momentum and life that is beautiful." Westwood here identifies how mutuality, rather than dominance, is at the heart of genuine church-community relationships. Such mutuality was a striking element of what was shared through the interviews drawn on above. It does not seem too strong to name this as "beautiful," and a foretaste of heavenly life.

Framework Assessment

In her in-depth evaluation of the *Reconciling Mission* program for the second cohort, Dr. Joanna Sadgrove noted an extensive range of projects, programs and partnerships that were generated, nurtured or strengthened during the participation period.[14] Sadgrove categorized these in two broad ways.

First were *projects that drew on the assets of a church building or grounds* which included:

- The initiation or development of regular community group activities, such as knit-and-natter groups, music workshops, and uniformed groups for young people.

- Social welfare provision, such as a school uniform bank, a community "silent" cinema for families, and lunch and hot meal clubs for the elderly other vulnerable groups.
- Eco Church and churchyard development projects.
- Work with neighbors to remodel the internal space of a church building to create a better community resource.

Second were *community-based partnership projects* which included:

- Work with the social prescriber of a local medical practice to support vulnerable families.
- Partnerships with local food banks and food co-operative schemes.
- Partnerships with diverse local organizations, including shops, city councils, arts organizations, voluntary association hubs, and schools, to address social issues.
- Work with Citizens UK, on local and national community-organizing.

Many of these commendable projects addressed core human needs, helping to overcome hunger, loneliness, isolation, and mental health issues. The *Reconciling Mission* theoretical model described in Chapter 1 identifies the value of moving beyond meeting such needs on the journey towards seeing more of the kingdom of heaven realized here on earth. If we focus on projects relating to this chapter's interviewees, Richard Westwood noted how St Anne's involvement in the Burntwood Be A Friend community project had prompted church members to be asking questions of why some people were going hungry or finding themselves homeless. This was moving them into the second stage of the model, raising questions of what was contributing to such inequalities in society, with church members wanting to explore these questions further and increase their awareness and understanding.

Some of the interviewees' projects had elements of challenging the system. The Men's Wellbeing Walk described by Esther Allen can be seen as part of the "talking revolution" identified in Chapter 1: at the heart of the wellbeing walk is mutual peer support. It therefore does not rely on health professionals to deliver a service, which is the predominant way the national healthcare system works in Britain. Rather it empowers local people to support one another in an informal and mutual process that avoids stigmatizing men with mental health struggles.

There were some similarities with Crafty Café, described by the Adamsons. They had specifically advertised the café as a space for those facing mental health struggles and as one that welcomed people with neurodiversity. As a result, such people were drawn in and found Crafty Café to be a safe space. Essential to the process was a sense of mutuality, with different people from the community sharing their craft activities with one another, along with the opportunity to join in conversation together around the table. This established a process with the potential to be "a communal growing for all involved," as Vicki Adamson put it, which challenges the prevailing—and hard-pressed—system of professional healthcare.

It is harder to assess where the church involvement in the gay pride event, Hay Pride, sits, as described by Luci Morriss and Ange Grunsell. At the heart of their church's motivation was a desire to communicate the acceptance of people of diverse sexualities, in contrast to the lack of acceptance conveyed by some in the wider church; and they wanted their church to contribute as a community partner alongside others. There was also an awareness-raising aspect to the overall event, which celebrates the contribution that people of diverse sexualities make to society. There may also be an element of challenging the system through trying to ensure that their voices are better heard. This was implied rather than explicitly named within the interview.

Given the 18-month timescale of the *Reconciling Mission* program, it is unsurprising that most of the projects influenced by the program were not part of creating major structural change in their local contexts. (An exception would be the community-organizing work with Citizens UK.)[15] Such change typically only occurs over a much longer period, possibly decades, and as part of a greater level of organization. Nevertheless, in different ways, each of the churches was involved in a process of seeing "the things God loves" being released and therefore seeing something of God's realm being better realized in their locality.

Dr. Joanna Sadgrove concluded her evaluation with this reflection:

> *These projects ranged in their audience and scale. Some were initiated during the national lockdowns and grew or developed during [participation in] the program in response to community needs. Most reflected the impact of networking with local organizations. Some involved high levels of congregational activity and collaboration; while others drew directly on the assets of church infrastructure. All indicated ways in which the deliberate and*

intentional engagement of the church with a local community, as fostered, encouraged, and supported by the Reconciling Mission *program, can stimulate and diversify how churches and Christians conceptualize and find new ways to participate in God's reconciling mission.*[16]

Biblical Reflection: Acts 4:5–12

If you or someone close to you has ever been silenced, excluded, or rejected at any stage because you or they are "different," then you or they will know what it feels like to be a stone that the builders rejected. If you or your friend received nasty comments, unfair judgments, or were made to feel invisible, then you or they will know what it is like to be a stone that the builders rejected. In which case you are, or someone you know is likely carrying hurt from that rejection. For how many of our neighbors, is this also true? The answer would likely trouble us, if we truly knew.

The apostle Peter understood this and had good news for his 1st-century listeners. Peter had witnessed that Jesus knew exactly what it was like to be a stone that the builders rejected. Jesus *is* the rejected stone. This rejection is at the heart of Jesus's story and experience. The good news that Peter shared with his audience was that, although rejected by men, Jesus had become the cornerstone on which God was building the community of God's people—and we might add has continued to do so over the last two thousand years. This means that, as one of the rejected stones, your friend or neighbor is going to be right next to the cornerstone that is Jesus.

There is a challenge offered by this story in Acts. The speaker is Peter, Petrus, the "rock" or "stone" in Greek. At first sight it may seem that Peter was pointing the finger of blame at the Jewish leaders of his day for having rejected Jesus and sanctioned his execution. He was certainly challenging them to wake up and notice what was going on. However, Peter would be mindful that only a few short weeks before this incident, on a traumatic night he was the one who had denied knowing Jesus when challenged by a young girl. He had rejected Jesus, when Jesus most needed a friend's support. Peter would therefore have known, at a deep and personal level, that he was called to embrace the stones that the builders rejected. As a foundation stone himself, he would have remembered that he was commissioned by Jesus to incorporate rejected stones into the community of God's people.

For those of us who are insiders in today's church, the challenge is this: how can we play our part in growing a local community which does better at incorporating and nurturing our neighbors who are different to us. For the pressing reality is that we need them on the team. Yet, sadly, too often the church has left our neighbors feeling that they do not really belong or are somehow—if only in subtle ways—inferior to us Christians.

In God's good economy, there are no first- and second-class citizens. Or, to change the metaphor, there is no one who is not good enough to play in the team. Rather, we need everyone on the team if we are to become a creative, dynamic, and flourishing local community. This means having honest conversations about what is damaging our local neighborhood. It means listening deeply to our neighbors. It also means opening up the space for them and encouraging them to bring all their gifts, skills, and contributions to shape our common life. God's realm will be better realized when all our neighbors can all stand tall, confident that they belong and can make their contribution.

The witness of participants in the *Reconciling Mission* program and their churches is that this is best achieved through finding ways to partner respectfully with our neighbors and local organizations. In doing so, these participants have found—as Peter proclaimed—that our salvation in Jesus is real, without forcing any of their neighbors to have to conform to a faith in the great rejected stone.

Questions for Reflection and Group Discussion

1 As you have read this chapter, which stories have most struck you, and why is that?

2 In what ways do you see your local church's missional engagement with her locality being echoed or inspired by the stories offered here? Are there ways in which you think your congregation(s) has gone beyond or deeper in her contextual engagement than these case study examples?

3 What steps do you want to see your local congregation(s) taking to be either more outward-looking, or more open to receiving the gifts of others outside the church and working in partnership with them, or readier to shift into being the guest in your neighborhood interactions? Which of these challenges offers the most pertinent "growing edge" for your church's current season?

3 Collaborating to Meet Community Needs in Arizona

Casa Grande is a rapidly growing city of some 60,000 residents located midway between Phoenix and Tucson in the Sonoran Desert of southern Arizona. During the temperate months, October through April, the city experiences significant influxes of both winter visitors and unhoused individuals. In recent decades thousands of immigrants have also passed through Casa Grande, due to its proximity to the US-Mexico border and to two major highways.

Seeds of Hope,[1] a nonprofit organization founded as a "Christian resource for community development," was launched in 1992 by the First Presbyterian Church of Casa Grande. Although the Seeds of Hope offices continue to be located on First Presbyterian's campus, the staff, board members, and volunteers come from multiple congregations in the area. Seeds of Hope programs are primarily offered through a community center on the west side of the city as well as a large downtown church building.

Seeds of Hope's philosophy was shaped by Dr. John Perkins, a leader in the formation of the Christian Community Development Association (CCDA).[2] Dr. Perkins famously identified the "Three Rs of Christian Community Development—Relocation, Reconciliation, and Redistribution." Dr. Perkins believed that people of faith should move into the most distressed neighborhoods in their community and begin to build relationships with their neighbors. Out of those relationships, he suggested, we could identify the "felt needs" of the residents and work with them to address those needs.

This is how those Three Rs took shape through Seeds of Hope in Casa Grande, as recounted by one of the authors, David, who also served as the first executive director of Seeds of Hope.

Seeds of Hope and the 3 Rs

After moving to Casa Grande in 1992 and assuming the role of executive director of Seeds of Hope, I spent a year working with a task force to identify a suitable neighborhood where my family and I could relocate. The task force recommended Cabana, then known as "the projects," on the north side of Casa Grande, and my spouse, Mert, and our year-and-a-half old son, Everett, and I moved there in January of 1994. Our second son, Emerson, was born in 1996 while we were living in Cabana.

We soon realized that there were three major problems in the Cabana neighborhood:

1. It was a 100% rental neighborhood, and studies consistently find that healthy neighborhoods are a mix of rental properties and owner-occupied homes.[3]
2. There were many children in the neighborhood, and parents reported that their children needed more structured activities after school and during the summer months.
3. Four of the 100 units were drug houses, which neighborhood children referred to as "crack houses." Drug sales were common, as was violence and the threat of drive-by shootings.

During the first year that we lived in the Cabana neighborhood the problems seemed to get worse, not better. We would regularly hear gunshots at night and so moved Everett's bed away from the window as his bedroom was in the front of the house. Our response to the violence was to build relationships and to pray; trusting that God and our neighbors would protect us. However, while we were indeed unharmed, nothing changed in Cabana itself.

One day the principal of the local elementary school, Doug Price, called me into his office. Principal Price was familiar with Seeds of Hope and aware that our family had moved into the Cabana neighborhood. As principal, he was receiving reports from his teachers that children in the local neighborhood were afraid to sleep at night because of the gunfire and threats of drive-by shootings. Mr. Price cared deeply about his students and knew they could not learn if they did not sleep well due to the threat of violence. He suggested the two of us meet with the manager of the Cabana Properties and the

Casa Grande Police Department. We were fortunate to have a supportive property manager and to connect with two committed police officers who understood what we were dealing with.

The efforts of this coalition—of a faith-based organization, a local elementary school, the brave manager of a housing complex, and the local police department—is what ultimately transformed the Cabana neighborhood into a safer mix of owner-occupied and rental properties. This coalition was supported by friends and community members, a support we needed when the neighbor kids reported that one of the drug gangs had targeted our house for a drive-by shooting … correctly suspecting that we were involved in the changes that were occurring in the neighborhood.

More than three decades later, relationships continue to be at the heart of Seeds of Hope ministries—whether through the Hot Lunch Program, diverse programs for children, youth, and adults at the Mondo Anaya Community Center, the Community Garden program, or the monthly free Medical Clinic. I remember telling my staff that Seeds of Hope was committed first and foremost to relationships, and that if a program contributed to relationship-building we would keep it, but if it did not, we would eliminate it. Community development starts with relationships.

The second "R" of Christian community development is "Reconciliation," and there are two components—vertical reconciliation with God and horizontal reconciliation with each other. At Seeds of Hope, we endeavored to embed this goal of a loving relationship with God and neighbor in all our programs. A Captain in the Salvation Army named Tom Ford was particularly helpful in meeting this goal, starting a weekly Bible study at the Hot Lunch program and infusing regular Bible studies into our after-school programs for children and youth. I saw lives transformed during my 12 years in Casa Grande because of this emphasis, as Captain Ford and I co-led a Seeds of Hope boys' club until I left the community in 2004.

The third "R" of Christian community development, in my adapted version, combines "redistribution" with "responsibility." This responsibility is also at two levels—personal and corporate. In other words, individuals must be responsible for themselves and their actions while at the same time practicing mutual responsibility—an understanding that we are all responsible for each other. I would cite two examples of how Seeds of Hope emphasized personal responsibility.

One of the first two programs of Seeds of Hope was "Project YES," which stood for "Youth Engaged in Service." This was a community service program designed for young people, both boys and girls, who had gotten into trouble with the law. With the strong support of the presiding juvenile judge, we established Project YES to put young offenders to work around the community, serving their "community service" hours, often ranging from 50 to 100 hours. Under the firm but loving supervision of a director and several volunteers, Project YES youth would clean up litter, paint out graffiti, and perform other service projects for nonprofit organizations, and for elderly or infirm members of the community.

Project YES was established on the principle of both individual responsibility and mutual responsibility. Individual youth were held accountable for their behavior, while at the same time the community assumed its responsibility towards the young people. Seeds of Hope provided a mechanism for these young people to complete their community service hours. They were each responsible for the misdeeds that got them into trouble; while as a community we collectively took responsibility for providing a way for them to "clean the slate" and start over.

A second early initiative, known as the Hot Lunch program, was the community's way of collectively saying: "We care about the hungry and homeless in our community, and we want to provide a hot meal for them every day that we can." Seeds of Hope agreed to start this program after a six-month listening process in which church and nonprofit leaders collectively called for such a program.

However, the responsibility did not just lie with the community to feed the hungry; we also wanted the participants to know that they were also responsible to contribute. We therefore established a "point system" whereby participants could eat each day but would also need to pitch in by cleaning tables, mopping the floor, or assisting in other ways. I knew the program was succeeding when a regular participant confronted a newcomer who was used to free food with no expectation to give back. "You don't just eat and run here," he told the newcomer, "You've got to help mop the floor like you said you would."

In sum, the process of Christian community development starts with relationship-building and with relocation. It doesn't always mean that we physically move from one neighborhood to another, but it does mean that we relocate ourselves out of our current comfort zone to where people are living who are different from us. After such relocation we can experience reconciliation—with God and with each other. The third "R" of Christian community development is redistribution and responsibility—first for oneself and one's own behavior and secondly for others and the community of which one is part.

Seeds of Hope was birthed in 1992 due to the leadership and resources of one congregation, First Presbyterian, the philosophy of a national organization, CCDA, and the support of multiple community leaders, both civic and religious. In more recent years the organization relocated the Community Center to a new neighborhood, grew to encompass many congregations, and helped birth a city-wide faith-based network called Faith Alliance.

Casa Grande's Faith Alliance provides a mechanism whereby the Protestant, Catholic, and Latter-Day Saints (LDS) religious communities in Casa Grande coordinate with each other along with nonprofit, government, and civic associations to meet basic human needs. A previous Seeds of Hope Director, Mark Vanderheyden, is broadly credited with leading the effort to establish the Faith Alliance.

Scott McEuen, one of the LDS leaders who is deeply involved with the Faith Alliance, described its formation:

> *I was one of the founders of what's called Faith Alliance of Casa Grande. We modeled it after one in Tempe, Arizona, and we did so because we admired the way their churches were working together. We sponsor various activities such as an annual blood drive that rotates from church to church. Our working together has built relationships.*

Local leaders believe that the Faith Alliance brings churches together, particularly through initiatives like the Interfaith Homeless Emergency Lodging Program (I-HELP). Participating churches "open their doors to the community and registered, unhoused individuals are able to seek shelter and get a safe night's sleep."[4]

Casa Grande's Faith Alliance may never end poverty and homelessness in the community, but the alliance has improved the coordination of services and the relationships among the city's religious community, nonprofit organizations, and government agencies. As Scott McEuen concluded, "everything we do is built on relationships."

There are both costs and benefits to congregations that significantly engage with their communities. The tangible costs are finances, time, and wear and tear on facilities. As Pastor Paul Elgin of First Presbyterian put it:

> *With an older demographic, especially in our session and our leadership, we have limited energy to do things like evangelism and stewardship and outreach. All of those are expensive in terms of resources and time commitment. For example, we pay half the salary of the Seeds of Hope Executive Director, and we provide office space and host fundraising dinners for Seeds of Hope.*

Nevertheless, pastors and other congregational members identified many more upsides than downsides stemming from their engagement with the community. Bill Heinle, Associate Pastor at First Presbyterian, described the benefits this way:

> *It's our identity, that Seeds of Hope is identified as something that grew out of First Presbyterian. I think the community sees the birth of Seeds of Hope coming primarily from the dreams and hopes of the members of First Presbyterian. And it had to start with the leadership, particularly Rev. Rick Lemberg, as Rick was a driving force in founding Seeds of Hope. The community identifies Seeds of Hope with First Presbyterian, even though we don't claim ownership, and many other congregations are now involved.*

Cindy Schaider, a member of First Presbyterian who is also active in the community, noted another benefit to the congregation of being visibly involved in its geographic location:

> *The congregation has grown, and there are younger families coming now and bringing children, so they've heard of us. They've heard that this is an active church and are becoming part of the congregation. We have women who participate in our yoga class that we host on our campus who are non-members of the church and who now also attend my Bible study. So, we're getting people due to our presence in the community.*

Lisa Navarro Fitzgibbons, current mayor and member of the local Catholic church, highlighted the value for the entire community of addressing the needs of the most vulnerable:

It's the understanding that we're all here for the common good and that we all have the same mission, to serve the people of our community. We all serve a common purpose. I think having those relationships and understanding and being open-minded has strengthened relationships. A lot of people have misconceptions about the homeless, but they're human beings and for whatever reason they are in the situation they are. The benefit to the congregation is it helps them see the common good and to see people as people.

Individual Motivations

Whether serving as staff, board members, or volunteers, individuals cited a variety of motivations for becoming involved in their local community. Many of those connected with Seeds of Hope or the Faith Alliance mentioned their faith as a primary motivator, such as Antonia Nunez, the Programs Manager for Seeds of Hope:

When I began the position as the Hot Lunch Coordinator I was just getting back into church and starting to raise my kids. Although I've raised my kids in the Catholic tradition, I found this role with Seeds of Hope very comfortable. And sometimes it didn't feel like it was work because we would do daily devotions at the Hot Lunch Program. And I just had to thank God because I realized, "I'm getting paid for this!" I'm getting to praise God and share God's love and show compassion to people who are overlooked in our community.

Mayor Lisa Navarro Fitzgibbons added a similar thought:

My faith plays a huge part because when I look at people, I feel like I'm looking at Jesus in their eyes. Every week at church they pray for the public servants and people that are setting policy. I tell my priest all the time, "I feel like you're looking right at me and saying, I'm praying for Lisa to make good decisions, to help people." So literally every week I take it seriously when they pray for public servants. And the prayers for those making decisions for the public are to make sure we take everyone into consideration.

Others reported that in addition to their faith their professional roles propelled them into the community. This is how Cindy Schaider described her journey:

> I came here right after graduating from college with a degree in public administration with an emphasis on corrections. And I intended to work in the juvenile corrections field. Instead, I got a job with a behavioral health agency and worked doing outpatient counseling and in the detox center and the Mental Health Crisis Stabilization Unit. That eventually evolved to me becoming a workshop provider, and that led me out into the community. I found that I was skilled at working well with others in the community and ran with it. Then I was able to sculpt my job into what I wanted to do, community engagement, by networking and community organization. The community organizing movement emerged in the late 1980s to help communities to organize to solve their own problems. Since we already had that community focus in place, it was natural to become a part of that movement. I became active in the community collaboration and development part of this community.

Former High School District Superintendent Scott McEuen expressed it this way:

> I've been president of Kiwanis Club, I've been president of the school board, I've been on the hospital board. It was natural because I was an administrator at the high school, so I joined the Rotary Club and the Kiwanis Club. It was a natural evolution because of my profession, I guess that's the best way to put it. When I retired, I realized, "This feels good to serve the community and to bring people together, to build bridges among the churches." I became even more involved in community activities and community affairs. And it started because of my profession. Serving in the community is important for everybody – for me, for our church, for the community.

Despite the overwhelming needs and the setbacks, those who are deeply involved in serving the community also reported great joy in that service. Antonia Nunez, the Director of Programs, said what gives her joy is:

> Helping people and seeing growth in those that really want it, such as seeing one of our peer leaders who grew up in a low-income household graduate from high school and get her first job at the Walmart pharmacy. She went on to college and then joined the Navy, as she wanted to travel the world. And then seeing some of the homeless come out of being homeless and being able to help them furnish their homes. It all happens in God's time. And then being able to help the parents, because we're basically the

> *bridge from the school to home. I run to many different schools because a student will have an issue at school, and we know mom doesn't get out of work until 5:30.*

The LDS leader and former school superintendent Scott McEuen responded this way:

> *I have built friendships from outside my church, because the majority of my friends are not in my church. There are many other churches and other organizations. I've established friendships and I've established relationships that are very rewarding. I like seeing our city grow in a good way, and it has certainly grown.*

Associate Pastor Bill Heinle noted the personal growth he has experienced through his work in the community:

> *By personality I am an introvert. But when I work with other people and form bonds, it's very sustaining for me. And being able to work on a project and see it through to a positive result is rewarding, to see some evidence of what you've accomplished. That's a change over my lifetime because I didn't start out that way; but working with others has helped me grow.*

The Limits of Compassion

Feeding the hungry, housing the homeless, and tutoring kids after school are all worthy efforts, but a common criticism is that such efforts do not address the root causes that drive such issues—such as systemic poverty, lack of affordable housing, under-resourced schools, racism, poor mental health, and addictions. Several individuals acknowledged that compassionate service alone may be inadequate to address deep structural inequities and individual dysfunctions.

Pastor Elgin of First Presbyterian suggested that the greatest challenge in community work is the overwhelming nature of local needs: "The fact that it just keeps coming every day and you can't ever fix it. Jesus said we'll always have the poor with us, but we're called to do what we can to help those who are nearby us. That is the second part of the verse that Jesus was quoting, 'therefore, care for the poor in your land.'"

Cindy Schaider, who served as Director of a Drug Prevention program for many years, acknowledged that prevention efforts are not always successful:

> *Recently I attended a funeral where we buried a local couple's daughter who died from an overdose of fentanyl at 25 years of age. I spent my entire professional life trying to prevent such tragedies. I imagined that I had a net, and I was in this rushing river trying to catch fish before they fell over a waterfall, but I missed one. And that one died, despite the fact that I spent my whole professional life trying to live our motto that we would not lose even one.... We probably prevented 2,500 from going over, but we missed that one, and that one died. At the funeral, Father Ariel said God was standing with her the day she died; she was never alone. We can think about all this academically, but when you get right down to it, this is a matter of life and death. This is real lives and real people, and people are hungry, are using, and people don't have a place to live. And it's life and death in every community. Those are powerful challenges.*

The Essential Work of Relationship-Building

Relationship-building requires commitment, time, mutuality, and reliability. As with any significant relationship—such as with a friend, romantic partner, or work colleague—building and maintaining community relationships will demand an investment of time from multiple parties. While often one party will initiate the relationship, the decision to also invest in the relationship will also require commitment from the responding party.

According to Arnold Toynbee, society itself is a system of relationships. Toynbee argued that, "The truth seems to be that a human society is, in itself, a relation: a particular kind of relation between human beings who are not only individuals but are also social animals in the sense that they could not exist at all ... without being in this social relation with one another."[5]

Likewise, every community is a system of relationships. Mack McCarter, the founder of Community Renewal International, suggests that "relationships are formed by what we share in common."[6] McCarter urges that we "re-villagize" our communities, noting that the only human collectivity that has not collapsed over time is the village. Empires rise and fall, and countries form and reform, but villages as entities persist—even if particular villages may be abandoned. In the context of a village, relationships are face-to-face and are built over time.

The key ingredient of successful relationships is trust, and McCarter proposes that, "the first task in rebuilding a culture of caring is to win trust."[7] Trust is accrued over time by demonstrating commitment to the relationship and through reliability in fulfilling one's commitments. When trusting relationships are already embedded in the culture of a particular community, the task of organizing coalitions to address community challenges is greatly facilitated. When trust is absent or precarious, however, the job of forming effective coalitions may prove fiendishly difficult, even impossible.

Casa Grande is a relatively young community, incorporated only in 1915—three years after Arizona was admitted as a state to the Union. The Presbyterian congregation in town was established earlier, in 1896, and known as Endeavor Church. The history of the congregation reflects the significant engagement of pastors and lay leaders in the community, including service on the City Council, local school boards, and service clubs. Many members were also prominent business owners in the Casa Grande community.[8]

By the time Rev. Rick Lemberg arrived in 1987, he was the beneficiary of nearly a century-long tradition of a congregation engaging deeply with its community. Pastor Lemberg built on that tradition by establishing multiple connections, including through coaching soccer and tennis teams, and by launching Seeds of Hope.

After 18 years of service to First Presbyterian Pastor Lemberg left to accept a pastoral call to a Presbyterian congregation in California. The City Council declared an "Appreciation Day" for Pastor Lemberg, and then-mayor Chuck Walton read the following statement:

> *Most ministers—and I don't blame them for doing this—have a tendency to herd their own flock and take care of their own. That's a tremendous responsibility and I can understand that. Tonight, we are going to say goodbye to a minister in Casa Grande who not only took care of the 99 of his flock but has also gone out to the rest of Casa Grande and counted us as the one. Rick Lemberg has had a tremendous influence on everybody in Casa Grande, especially the youth ....*[9]

The mayor's statement specifically credited Pastor Lemberg's role in envisioning Seeds of Hope. The nonprofit organization benefitted not only from the funding and facilities provided by First Presbyterian, but also from the church's reputation in the community.

As the founding executive director of Seeds of Hope, I spent my first six months in the role meeting with community leaders—including pastors, nonprofit executives, and city officials—to discuss community needs and existing assets and how this new nonprofit might respond. Almost without exception, I was received warmly and granted a surprising degree of trust. The reason likely had little to do with me and much more to do with the reputation of First Presbyterian and its leadership, including Rev. Rick Lemberg.

Coalition-building is a form of relationship-building, and thus also depends on the trust and reliability of the parties involved. In the case of Seeds of Hope, a congregation's legacy of community involvement, combined with a pastor's demonstrated commitment to community engagement, proved an effective launch ramp for a new nonprofit organization with a mission to serve the community.

Not every congregation can claim a century of significant community engagement, nor be blessed with a senior minister with a passion to serve in the community. Yet the principles identified in the Casa Grande case study are relevant to every congregation embedded in a particular community.

Learnings

As a small city with a history of collaborative relationships, Casa Grande was well positioned to support locally grown nonprofit organizations like Seeds of Hope as well as broader associations like the Faith Alliance. There are several lessons from this community that are relevant for communities of all sizes, as follows.

1 *Leadership.* Each of the individuals interviewed credited one or more leaders who sparked a new organization or initiative. Rev. Rick Lemberg, a former Senior Minister of First Presbyterian, envisioned Seeds of Hope.

Mark Vanderheyden, a previous Seeds of Hope executive director, championed the Faith Alliance. Craig McFarland, former Mayor of Casa Grande, created a task force on homelessness that morphed into the I-HELP network. In every instance, the leadership of one or more individuals was critical in the successful efforts to meet community needs.

2 *Christian Faith.* Whether Roman Catholic, Protestant, or Latter-Day Saints, the interviewees stressed that their service to the community emerged from and was sustained by their Christian faith. Working side-by-side in various community activities also strengthened the relationships among those of differing faith traditions. For example, members of a local Baptist congregation gained respect and appreciation for LDS young people who volunteered with them in the after-school program at the Seeds of Hope community center.

3 *Outward Focus.* Several of the community leaders highlighted that one of the greatest values of community service was the "outward focus" it encouraged among members. Scott McEuen reported that his core philosophy is to "make sure the doors swing outward, not swing in"—looking outward to engage with and serve the broader community.

4 *Relationships.* Most significantly, community leaders consistently pointed to the trusting relationships that already existed across the community as key to successful collaboration. This included both *bonding* capital, within congregations and other organizations, and *bridging* capital, among the congregations, nonprofit organizations, city government, and service clubs.[10] As Scott McEuen emphasized earlier, "everything is built on relationships."

Framework Assessment

Referencing the typology in Chapter 1, we would identify Seeds of Hope and the Faith Alliance as primarily operating to meet basic human needs. At the same time, collaborating to address such needs has also served to raise awareness of injustice among those serving the community. Whether such awareness will ultimately lead to challenging and transforming unjust systems is yet to be determined.

Community is built when people come together to identify their needs and develop creative responses to meet them. Casa Grande offers an example of a collaborative community that leverages existing assets and relationships to meet basic human needs. In the next chapter we will examine Milwaukee Inner-city Congregations Allied for Hope (MICAH), a faith-based organization in Milwaukee, Wisconsin, that organizes to advocate for systemic change and justice.

Biblical Reflection: Mt 25:31–46 and Beyond

In Matthew's gospel Jesus offers us a provocative parable which many Christians have taken as a mandate for providing services that meet basic human needs. The parable suggests that Jesus closely identifies himself with the hungry, the stranger or immigrant, the sick, and the prisoner; and that actions to feed those who hunger, to welcome those who are estranged, to care for those who are sick, and to visit those who are imprisoned, are all actions that are done as if to him personally.

It is therefore not surprising that the early Christian communities were known for their ministries in both word and deed, such as economic sharing. (Acts 4:32–37) Nor is it surprising that the apostle Paul plays a key role in gathering a collection of money from around the eastern Roman Empire to take to the Christians in Jerusalem who were facing economic hardship, and that a number of his letters urge the church to which he writes to be generous in giving to this fund. (e.g. 2 Cor. 8 & 9)

When it came to simply sharing a meal together as Christian believers, it seems clear from early church practices that they expected table fellowship to happen regularly across the social and economic strata of the society. When this failed to happen properly and fairly, the apostle Paul, for one, was quick to challenge the early church. (1 Cor. 11:17–34) Likewise the apostle James, probably the brother of Jesus, was quick to criticize Christian believers who succumbed to society's distinctions based on wealth. (Jas. 2:1–13) Further, James claimed that faith without deeds was meaningless, citing the sharing of food and clothing with those who were in need as evidence of a real faith. (Jas. 2:14–26)

Many have critiqued "charitable" ministries, arguing that they serve to prop up unjust and failing institutions rather than to transform them. Rather than preferring the Matthew 25 parable, such faith-based advocates may prefer the prophet Micah's call: "He has told you, O mortal, what is good, and what does the Lord require of you but to do justice and to love kindness and to walk humbly with your God?" (Mic. 6:8) There is an understanding that "doing justice" requires more than just charitable acts.

The author and practitioner Dennis Jacobson urges that congregations avoid providing direct services and focus instead on "Congregation-Based Community Organizing." Jacobson argues that "social change is the product of power applied effectively in the public arena."[11] Nonetheless, Jacobson proposes that community organizers should organize people around their self-interest ... which is another way of describing felt needs. In responding to a community's or a neighborhood's felt needs, the most important questions may be to ask: "Who is defining the felt needs?" and "Whose needs are not being met?"

There is nothing inherently wrong with congregational or institutional leaders defining needs and designing programs to meet them. Such programs recruit volunteers, build relationships, and meet very real individual needs for such basics as food, clothing, and housing. The testimony of the case studies offered in this book is that genuine transformation is most likely to occur when a particular neighborhood or community organizes to assess its own needs and collaborates together to meet them and organizes to change the structures which prevent those needs being fairly met.

Questions for Reflection and Group Discussion

1 Collaboration is a valued "asset" in the Casa Grande community. What are some significant assets, strengths, or gifts in your community?
2 Meeting basic human needs is typically an important starting point for congregations that are engaging their communities. Who are some of the significant providers of such needs in your community, and what is your congregation's relationship with them?

3 As offered in Chapter 1, a next step beyond meeting basic needs is often to raise one's awareness of what is causing injustice and then to look at challenging the system. To what degree are congregations or faith-based coalitions in your community also engaged in such work or activities?

4 Raising Awareness and Pursuing Justice in Wisconsin

Milwaukee, Wisconsin, is a post-industrial city of about half a million residents located in the upper midwestern region of the United States. In 1960 the city's population was nearly 750,000, but due to the decline of its industrial and agricultural processing base Milwaukee experienced significant population loss. Milwaukee's remaining population of some 500,000 is diverse, with Blacks and Whites each comprising nearly 40 percent of the city's population.[1]

As with many other US cities in the American Midwest the last half century, Milwaukee hemorrhaged those jobs that paid decent wages and offered benefits. Well-paying jobs are limited, housing stock is aging, and systemic racism and functionally segregated neighborhoods are a reality. As resident Earl Ingram, Jr., lamented, "I wish young people had the opportunity that my generation in Milwaukee had—the highest standard of living for Black people in this nation. You need to understand the magnitude of what it meant when people took those middle-class jobs away."[2]

Milwaukee Inner-City Congregations Allied for Hope (MICAH)

Amid Milwaukee's multi-decade decline, religious leaders in the city came together in 1988 to found MICAH—Milwaukee Inner-City Congregations Allied for Hope. Comprised today of more than 40 member congregations—including Jewish, Christian, Muslim, Buddhist, and Unitarian Universalist—MICAH's primary purpose is "to empower people to act together in pursuit of justice."[3] MICAH is a member of a grassroots organization known as WISDOM, a statewide coalition "dedicated to bringing diverse communities together to advocate for justice through community organizing."[4] It is also part of Gamaliel, a national organization founded to "train community and faith leaders in building political power and creating organizations that unite people of diverse faiths."[5]

MICAH is an interfaith organization focused on raising awareness, advocating for change, and organizing the community around issues of justice. MICAH's priorities have evolved over the decades as needs emerged and changed. Recent initiatives have addressed criminal justice and prison reform, education and health, jobs and economic development, racial equity, and transportation. As a response to the rise in Christian nationalism the last decade, MICAH launched a "We All Belong" campaign which seeks to both "protect democracy" and "build the beloved community."[6]

Retired Lutheran Pastor Joe Ellwanger, one of the founders of MICAH, moved to Milwaukee in 1967 from Birmingham, Alabama, where he had pastored an African American congregation from 1958 to 1967.[7] He remembers those nine years as, "the height of the civil rights movement," with the center of that movement in Birmingham and nearby Selma. While in Alabama Pastor Ellwanger marched alongside leaders such as Dr. Martin Luther King, C.T. Vivian, Andrew Young, and James Lawson. He describes them as, "Christian pastors who had it in their bones that justice work is what God is calling us to do."

Pastor Ellwanger recalls that Dr. King observed that while white racism in the South was blatant, racism in the North was just as pernicious if less overt.[8] Pastor Ellwanger agrees that today racism is as real in the northern US as it is in the southern US. The difference he sees is that in the South, Blacks and Whites interact routinely and often live across the street from each other, whereas the reality in the North is "de facto segregation," where Whites and Blacks have fewer neighborly encounters with one another.

In Alabama, Pastor Ellwanger learned "that justice work is not an add-on for the people of God, but an essential part of living the gospel. That's where I saw clearly that doing justice is part of loving neighbor and living the gospel. I could not leave that out of my work or my calling as a pastor."

Rev. Marilyn Miller has also been part of MICAH since its inception and was a member of the Lutheran congregation in Milwaukee that Pastor Ellwanger led. She served as a past president of MICAH, and on multiple MICAH committees. Rev. Miller spoke of her experience of working for justice in Milwaukee, noting that she grew up just three blocks away from the church where Joe Ellwanger pastored. She remembers that his congregation went into the neighborhood to invite people to come to their programs, and that Pastor Ellwanger lived out his beliefs.

> *That's what he preached. That's what he taught and lived out. He resided in the community. To be effective, you had to be out in the community, and working with the community. You had to be addressing the issues in the community, not just be about "us in the church."*

Pastor Ellwanger and Rev. Miller both believe that while individual congregations appropriately respond to basic human needs in their surrounding neighborhoods, MICAH should stay focused on *raising awareness* of the underlying reasons for those needs and advocating for changes in systems. Rev. Miller states, "That is where MICAH is called to act because it's the underlying issues that the average person doesn't see. They don't see the underlying issues of joblessness and injustice, and how that produces food insecurity and affects people's sense of worth."

Individual Motivations

Those in current or recent leadership roles in MICAH include Lisa Jones, the former executive director and lead organizer, as well as President Dr. Richard Shaw and Vice President Rev. Joseph Jackson. Dr. Shaw and Rev. Jackson each lead predominantly African American congregations in the city of Milwaukee, and Ms. Jones is a lifelong city resident. This is how former Director Jones describes her motivation for becoming an advocate for justice and a community organizer.

> *I got into organizing work when Jay Anderson was killed by the Wauwatosa police. At that time, I lived in Milwaukee about a half a mile away from the park where Jay was killed. That was my entrée into justice work. I asked myself, "What am I going to do? Another black man gets killed by the police … am I going to do something?" I believe that we can pray, but I also started to do a lot of preaching as I'm a lay minister in my own United Methodist tradition. I can no longer stay personally silent for people's comfort while there is oppression.*
>
> *In 2017 I joined a campaign called "Close MSDF," which is the Milwaukee Secured Detention Facility. We were primarily black female organizers working on policing and supporting the Anderson family, and through that work I came to realize the high incarceration rate of black males. That's what*

motivated me to say that we need to not only address concerns about policing but also look at the incarceration rate. I went to the campaign meetings, and I met a number of people like Pastor Joe Ellwanger. And then I participated in organizing training through the WISDOM Network.

The main thing that pushed me forward was God saying, "I'm sending you forth." It's up to me to either answer the call or not. But it was put there before me, and I chose to answer the call when God was tapping my shoulder to do it.

Like Pastor Ellwanger, the current president of MICAH, Dr. Richard Shaw, also has Alabama roots. Dr. Shaw describes his calling into justice work as follows:

I was born and raised in Marion, Alabama, a small town right outside of Selma. And my mother marched with Dr. Martin Luther King. But coming from a small town in Alabama to engage in urban ministry was a culture shock for me. Back in 2012, a report was released regarding disparities in mass incarceration in Wisconsin, and when that came out some pastors from MICAH reached out to me. We established an initiative on mass incarceration that got me involved and brought me in.

Rev. Joseph Jackson, vice president of MICAH, recounts that his journey into community ministry came by virtue of his calling to become a pastor.

My involvement in MICAH goes back to its founding, which was in 1988. I was a member at Providence Baptist Church, and my pastor was one of the seven pastors that founded MICAH. When I was called to my first pastorate at Evergreen Church, they were already a MICAH church. There was no need to lead a church into social justice work in MICAH, as they were already there. There was no question that we would do community work with a social justice lens in that particular community.

Brother Will Perry, the former executive director of the Milwaukee Islamic Dialogue Center, a MICAH member institution, credits his family and his faith for creating an ethic of service that propelled him into community work.

It started with my adoptive father serving me and sheltering me and my mother and then it went from there. My adoptive father was a Marine back in the Korean War. After finishing high school, I also joined the Marine Corps Reserve Unit here in Milwaukee. I followed his lead in terms of being of service to this country for six years as a reservist, and then I served for 27 years with the Milwaukee Fire Department.

One of the pillars of Islam is that we belong to the community of humanity, so we're obligated to be of service. A Muslim should be someone that's welcoming to others. He or she should be someone who is concerned about their fellow human beings. Which means we're there when we're needed, to the best of our ability within the requirements of Islam and our Prophet Muhammad, peace and blessings be upon him.

Based on these four examples, we see that the prodding to engage in community activism can emerge from a specific crisis, such as death of an unarmed citizen; a pressing issue, like mass incarceration; a particular leadership role, such as pastor of a community-minded congregation; or from the values of one's family and belief system, such as a faith in Islam. However, while there are many routes into community engagement, the key for these individuals was the presence of an existing organization that channeled their energy and activism.

Compassion and Justice

Unlike Seeds of Hope and the Faith Alliance in Casa Grande, Arizona, in Chapter 3, MICAH does not provide direct services that meet basic human needs. However, many individual member congregations do, as Brother Perry, formerly of the Milwaukee Islamic Dialogue Center, describes:

Although this is a place of Muslim worship, it's also a place of community for families that are not Muslim. We have an exceptional food pantry here, working with other larger food organizations. We've now been operating for almost 20 years, and last year we served over a million pounds of food, reaching maybe 25,000 families. We go to various locations around the city to serve people in other neighborhoods that can't get to ours. We help people from all over the city, no matter whether they're Muslim or not.

Rev. Marilyn Miller explained that while MICAH does not offer compassionate ministries such as providing food and clothing, MICAH raises awareness, advocates for change, and organizes the community. Rev. Miller offered the example of a family in a MICAH-affiliated congregation whose young son had extremely high levels of lead in his blood and was diagnosed with attention deficit disorder. While congregational members focused on supporting the boy and his family, congregational and MICAH leaders also saw the crisis as an opportunity to address the larger issue of lead exposure in the community.

The result was the formation of a Coalition On Lead Emergency (COLE) that includes about 30 organizations with a vision to "create a sustainable, lead-safe Milwaukee."[9] The mother of the lead-impacted boy from Rev. Miller's congregation is now paid to organize other parents. According to Rev. Miller, "organizing, done right, empowers people to act who otherwise did not see the possibility of making any difference in the community." Raising awareness and advocating for change are essential steps, but action only occurs when a community is mobilized, and leaders emerge.

Key to the organizing model MICAH employs is the presence of "core teams" in each member congregation. The core teams are attentive to local issues in their own neighborhoods and are also responsive to city-wide issues, such as lead exposure, around which MICAH organizes. According to Pastor Ellwanger, an effective core team does not need to be large: "The ideal is the pastor and four or five laypersons that really get it and work with the pastor. Even if the pastor leaves, you've got some people there that are going to make sure that the campaign continues."

The pastors with leadership roles within MICAH also noted the impact on their local congregations of MICAH's resourcing. As Rev. Jackson explained, "We receive training and tools from MICAH that we can use not only in the community but also as we organize ministries within the church." Rev. Jackson noted that congregational meetings became more structured and productive as congregational members learned skills from their participation in MICAH's meetings.

Dr. Shaw also described the benefit to his congregation of its participation with MICAH, "because those who feel called to live out their ministry and do the work of justice can find the opportunity here." He gave the example of a parishioner who worked closely with MICAH on prison reform, an issue she felt strongly about given that two of her sons were in that system. The congregation's relationship with MICAH provided an avenue for her to pursue a passion for change.

Not all MICAH initiatives for justice are swiftly embraced by every member congregation. Pastor Ellwanger offered the example of a resolution MICAH drafted to submit to the City Council for the "Everyone Belongs" campaign designed to counter Christian nationalism. While all the congregations supported language regarding the multi-faith nature of the community, several balked at a phrase that included differing gender identities.

Pastor Ellwanger worked to convince leaders from those congregations that, "when we *say* we all belong, then we have to mean we *all* belong." However, not everyone was convinced. "It helped me to abide—to stay in relationship," Pastor Ellwanger mused, "even when we disagree." His commitment to stay in relationship amid profound disagreement emerged from a love of those with whom he disagreed and from his own understanding of what it means to follow Jesus. "There's risk-taking involved in this work, as there was throughout Jesus's life. We who claim to follow Christ must take risks. Some people are going to disagree with us, just like some were always mad at Jesus," Pastor Ellwanger concluded.

Leadership for Change

Leadership opportunities and development thus occur at three levels in MICAH's faith-based community work:

- within the congregational core teams,
- within MICAH itself as an umbrella organization, and,
- within the issue-focused coalitions MICAH joins which emerge and disband over time.

However, traditional pastoral and lay leadership formation models are insufficient for the leadership requirements of congregations that engage their communities. Most ministerial leadership training focuses on preparing ministers to preach well and to provide pastoral care. In recent decades the rise of megachurches has also propelled demand for training in entrepreneurial leadership skills.

According to Alan Roxburgh and Fred Romanuk, something beyond the leader as pastor and the leader as entrepreneur is needed for today's missional ministry: "Leadership is about cultivating an environment that innovates and releases the missional imagination present among a community of God's people."[10]

Much like a farmer or gardener who prepares the soil, the cultivating leader attends to the environment, or culture, of the congregation. "The key to missional change is innovating an adaptive culture," according to Roxburgh and Romanuk.[11] The leader's primary task is less to "lead the charge" into the community than to equip the culture and the congregants to engage the community with curiosity and care. Effective leaders will therefore model such engagement while also inviting other members to likewise engage.

Such community-engaged leaders need to maintain both an internal and an external focus. The internal life of the congregation will continue to demand the attention of the minister, as the needs of congregational members for meaningful worship, faith development, pastoral care, and denominational connection will continue undiminished. At the same time, the needs of community members for allies in their quest for a safe and flourishing neighborhood will invite partnerships with congregations and faith-based organizations like MICAH.

How ministers and lay leaders balance these competing demands from congregational members and community members may determine the success of a congregation's foray into community engagement. Rev. Jackson acknowledges an initial tension among congregational members between their commitment to their Baptist tradition and their commitment to MICAH and their neighborhood.

> *They initially felt threatened about affiliating with MICAH because we also belong to the State Convention and some folks thought that we were choosing one over the other. They worried that I was going to pull us out of the Convention, and we were going to just simply do MICAH work, rather than be a part of the Convention and have MICAH as another ministry in our church. I had to demonstrate that it's possible both to be loyal to our Baptist tradition and to be engaged in our community.*

Today the congregation's Vision Statement captures the multiple commitments that Rev. Jackson identified: "To establish a church community in which the body has arms that reach within and without to meet the spiritual, physical, emotional and religious needs of the community."

In addition to balancing internal and external commitments, community-engaged leaders will also face the challenge of serving both as agents of *stability* and agents of *change* in their congregational systems. Douglas Powe and Lovett Wheems propose that successful change efforts require both "sustainers," or agents of stability, and "innovators," or agents of change. This is because "successful and lasting change comes more through evolution than revolution."[12]

Balance is required, as every congregation has a limited absorption capacity when it comes to its ability to incorporate change. Introducing disruptive change into a fragile system can overwhelm the system's ability to adapt, leading to outright rejection of the new initiative or even to collapse of the existing system. Powe and Wheems note that congregants expect spiritual grounding, "vital worship," and pastoral care from their leaders. If these three expectations are not met, then the internal life of the congregation will suffer. The challenge, therefore, is to meet the spiritual and formational needs of the congregation while also expanding members' vision to serve the broader community.

There are thus two polarities that leaders of community-engaged congregations must confront. The first is how to manage both the internal and the external demands of the ministry. The second is how to introduce genuine change—which is therefore disruptive—into a congregational system while maintaining sufficient resiliency to absorb the change.

Disruption and development, or challenge and change, are often conjoined. If agents of change want to create something new, they can expect to face resistance from something that is already established. At the same time, in every community there are practices that need to be sustained, while there are other aspects that need to be changed or transformed.

This unique ability—to balance internal and external demands and to combine disruptive actions with sustaining ones—are the hallmarks of effective leaders. Yet very few individual leaders can manifest all these qualities alone. What is most needed is a leadership *team* that collectively encompasses an internal and an external focus and combines disruptive with sustaining actions.

Nor can we rely only on ordained clergy to bring the full range of needed capacities. Rather, some clergy and lay members will be drawn primarily to internal and sustaining ministries, while others will be drawn primarily to external and disruptive ministries. Finding the necessary balance between these callings—respecting the fact that there are differing needs and callings—may be the key to successful polarity management.

Learnings

Leadership is thus a key ingredient for successful community engagement. This is not the leadership of a lone ranger. It is rather the leadership of a team of leaders, who collectively understand that multiple gifts, skills, and passions are needed. The following range of gifts and skills aims to summarize those that are most required:

1. The skill of *community building*. This skill values deep social capital and understands that congregational members need first to connect with each other. It brings people together and encourages connections among congregational members through a variety of formal and informal mechanisms.
2. The passion of *community advocacy*. This passion urges congregational members to look outward, and models that commitment through involvement in the community. This passion invites those in the congregation eager to work for justice to join community organizations with similar goals.
3. The gift of *disruption*. This courageous gift not only names what is not working in the congregation and community but actively disrupts it. It organizes marches, petitions, and other actions that disrupt the normal flow of systems that are oppressive and dysfunctional.
4. The gift of *sustaining*. This gift knows that change will only be sustainable if it's incorporated into existing systems. This gift brings an evolutionary, rather than a revolutionary, approach to systemic change, mainly because it wants to see the change be sustained rather than overturned.

All these gifts, skills, and passions—of community building, community advocacy, disruption, and sustaining—are necessary for successful change. The challenge is to convince those on either end of the polarity that the gifts, skills, and passions of those on the opposite end of the polarity are equally necessary.

Framework Assessment

Reflecting on the five-stage model introduced in Chapter 1, MICAH is firmly located in stages two and three—raising awareness of injustice and challenging the system. The ultimate goal of their efforts is to achieve stage four—system transformation. The core teams in each member congregation work to highlight injustice and to recruit the people and resources needed to address the injustice. MICAH staff and board leaders, along with partner organizations, then organize a collective voice, to challenge systems and strive for transformation.

MICAH has thrived since 1998 due to its ability to assemble religious congregations from multiple traditions in a coalition that pursues justice for all of Milwaukee's residents. MICAH's leadership emerges from local congregations and includes clergy and lay members who are rooted in their congregations who also feel compelled to serve their community. MICAH's accomplishments—ranging from criminal justice reform to public health improvement—demonstrate that congregational leaders who can balance an internal and an external focus are able to guide their congregants in contributing to the transformation of a community.

Biblical Reflection: Acts 19

With the decline of Christendom, Christianity is returning to its 1st-century roots as a living movement that must be nurtured at the margins of society. According to Terry Coy, the church in North America is in the process of returning to the margins due to "the collapse of Christendom, the fading of American civil religion, and the apparent triumph of secularization."[13] If Christians are able to embrace such an understanding, it will help them to recognize that the Christian church is no longer an institution that must be maintained at the center of society.

An organized religion that occupies significant space at the center of a society needs only to be maintained. Religious practice at the margins, by contrast, exists in a contested environment. Disruption of the status quo and an external focus are necessary strategies if such a movement is to survive.

Recorded in Acts 19, the experience of the apostle Paul and his entourage in the city of Ephesus offers a glimpse of what can transpire when an existing system is disrupted. Paul lived in Ephesus for more than two years, having discussions "daily" in a public lecture hall and performing "extraordinary miracles." (Acts 19:9–10) However, the success of Paul's ministry disrupted the existing system of worshipping Artemis, as new Christian adherents abandoned her worship in favor of following the Way.

This disruption threatened not only the religious foundation of the city but also the livelihood of the local artisans who crafted silver shrines of Artemis. The economic threat compelled a leading silversmith named Demetrius to organize a meeting of the affected workmen, which devolved into a two-hour long riot that sent the "whole city into an uproar." (Acts 19:32) Ultimately the city clerk was able to quiet the crowd, in part by affirming the greatness of Artemis. The clerk then urged Demetrius and his fellow craftsmen to take their grievances to a court of law.

We might wonder what the economic impacts might be of a widespread radical Christian discipleship practiced across the US—in contrast to the "Christian nationalism" which appears to prevail in parts of the church at present.

Questions for Reflection and Group Discussion

1 What life experiences have led you (and others, if a group) to become engaged in your community?

2 What issues or challenges in your community most lend themselves to being addressed through changes in public policy or other actions by elected officials? What collective action by your congregation and your neighbors might help to bring about necessary policy action?

3 How would you describe the relationships between leaders or members of your congregation and public decision-makers in your community? What would it look like to invest more intentionally in those relationships?

5 Neighborhood-Based Community Development in Montana

Billings is the largest city in the state of Montana with a population of about 120,000. Located in south-central Montana, Billings lies north of the Apsáalooke (Crow) Nation and west of the Tsis tsis'tas (Northern Cheyenne) Nation. Demographically, Billing's population is about 80 percent White, with the remainder primarily identifying as Native American, Hispanic, or Multiracial.[1] The major industries in Billings are agriculture, energy, education, and healthcare, with the city's diverse economy producing a consistently low unemployment rate.[2]

As with many communities, however, the benefits of a robust economy are not evenly distributed. Pervasive unemployment and poverty in the nearby Native American nations drive some tribal members into Billings in search of food and housing. The South Side of the city, stereotypically located "south of the tracks," enjoys greater racial diversity but also endures a median household income that is significantly lower than that of the city as a whole.[3]

Community Leadership and Development Incorporated (CLDI)

The movement that became the Community Leadership and Development Incorporated (CLDI) began with a group of young Christians in the late 1970s who asked, "What would it look like if a bunch of us moved together to this community (the South Side) and loved one another and the Lord?"[4] Their commitment to love God and neighbor propelled a dedication to the South Side neighborhood that continues to the present.

Several initiatives emerged from the location alongside their South Side neighbors, particularly from the relationships with neighborhood children and teenagers. One was a weight room, established in an abandoned grocery store. Another was Koinonia Mexican Restaurant, which one of the young newcomers described as "a Mexican restaurant with a Greek name run by a bunch of white guys who didn't know what they were doing."[5] A third initiative welcomed neighborhood children for a Friday morning breakfast. In the words of Scott Lynch, one of the young adults who moved into the South Side in the late 1970s, "We would do anything that would build relationships."[6]

Today CLDI's annual operating budget is nearly $3 million (£2.4 million), and the organization employs some 20 professional staff members.[7] More than half of those employees live in the South Side neighborhood. In 2017 CLDI undertook a $3.5 million (£2.8 million) renovation project to establish its headquarters building on the northern edge of the South Side, which includes meeting space for events and religious gatherings. The organization also renovated an old gas station across from the headquarters building to create the Rail//Line Coffee shop.[8]

As a faith-based nonprofit organization focused on a specific neighborhood, CLDI believes in "transforming lives on the South Side one relationship at a time."[9] CLDI offers a variety of programs in the neighborhood—including affordable housing, youth engagement, leadership development, job training, discipleship, and community development. CLDI also manages Hannah House, "a recovery home for women coming from incarceration or recovering from an addiction [that provides] a safe place for recovery and restoration of families."[10]

CLDI's Koinonia Management Company (KMC) manages more than 100 housing units, including 75 detached units on the South Side. KMC's goal is to provide quality affordable housing by working closely with the city's public housing authority and utilizing federal government housing vouchers. Patti Webster, the CEO of Billings' public housing authority known as Homefront, observes that "CLDI brings a spirit of hope and dignity to its work with our community's most vulnerable residents."

CLDI's Youth Works program aims to build relationships with students, primarily those in middle school (ages 11 to 14). According to the Youth Works Director, John Geiger, "our hopes are to build lasting relationships with students and to point them to Jesus." Leadership development occurs through a structured year-long internship program, and job training and economic development through the Rail//Line Coffee shop. CLDI views the Rail//Line Coffee shop as "restorative economic development," with the goal to "create new job opportunities and pave the way for new businesses to move into our community."[11]

An invitation to explore *Christian discipleship*—encouraging community members and program participants to follow Jesus—is infused throughout all CLDI's activities and programs. This focus was baked into the core culture of CLDI, as the founders were "passionate about Jesus and discipleship."[12] A meta goal of the diverse efforts in affordable housing, youth engagement, leadership development, job training, and addiction recovery is thus for individuals to explore a faith journey. While CLDI is not a church, it partners with local congregations and encourages individual faith development.

A second overarching purpose of CLDI's presence in the South Side is *community development*. CLDI seeks to accomplish this through supporting local institutions such as schools, providing employment opportunities, increasing home ownership, and creating community gathering spaces such as the Rail//Line Coffee shop. Community development is understood by CLDI not just as economic development, but as community empowerment and community flourishing.

As we saw in Chapter 3 in Casa Grande, Arizona, meeting basic human needs is often an essential starting point for congregations engaging their communities. Chapter 4, with a case study from Milwaukee, Wisconsin, highlights the value of raising awareness of injustice and challenging the system. CLDI in Billings, Montana, is primarily focused on leveraging change through community development in a specific place, the South Side neighborhood.

Individual Motivations

While CLDI employees report a range of motivations for committing to community development work, nearly all highlight their Christian faith. Many also cite the significance of a mentor who encouraged them in community ministry. Several participated in CLDI programs prior to being hired in a staff role. The Hannah House Director, Jessica Smith, first came to Hannah House as a resident, as she explains:

> *I lived in Hannah House as a resident, and that is where I learned the importance of community. They say, "the opposite of addiction is connection," and that's*

what Hannah House offers. You have a tight knit community there, but they push you to find community outside of the House as well.

My faith grew exponentially when I lived in the House. They would do Bible studies all the time, and that's what my recovery reflected. I've become a person constantly wanting to know more, and that's because of Hannah House.

I also had a great mentor, the previous Executive Director's wife. I don't think I could have had a better mentor. We were doing a Bible study in the summer of 2020, and that is when the previous director was getting ready to move on. My mentor encouraged me to pursue the position. I never would have put myself in the position of director – it was completely a calling from God.

John Geiger, the Youth Works Director, described a turbulent path that led him to CLDI and gave him a deep empathy for youth who are struggling themselves:

Twenty years ago, I had hit rock bottom in my addiction, had burned all my bridges, and had no family. I had become a person that I would despise. And a friend knew about a rehab program at the Dream Center in Los Angeles.[13] When I graduated from that program, I continued to do ministry with kids in that community.

When my wife and I got married we knew we wanted to do inner city ministry. We didn't know what that looked like, but we felt a conviction that we should live in the neighborhood where we're going to serve. Eric Basye, the former Executive Director of CLDI, invited us to come and work in the South Side neighborhood of Billings.

Part of what drew me into this work was my own life experience. And part of it was compassion or empathy for kids and others that I saw were struggling. I'd say that I was a good kid that had a dysfunctional background. I just fell onto the wrong side of the fence. There were some pivotal stages in my life that, had the right person come along, I might not have had to go through some of the junk I went through. I want to be the right person for others.

The stories of both Jessica and John are resonant of the detour in Moses's early life. God would not have chosen a life of addiction for either of them, and thus might be seen as a detour for both of them. Journeying into the life of Hannah House and the Dream Center offered paths of returning to a more fulfilled life. God was able to reintegrate their detours into meaningful ministry in support of others who had taken similar detours, and who needed to find a way through to a healthier life. Their detours turned into a gift for others, through God's gracious work.

While empathy for someone's experience of poverty or addiction is one gateway into community work, a personal Christian faith is also a consistent source of motivation for many CLDI employees. This is the case for Kaylee Thompson, the Internship Director at CLDI.

> *One summer when I was a student in college, I participated in a mini-internship at the Portland Rescue Mission, a facility for unhoused residents, in Oregon. I gained a desire to be involved with ministry and became aware that there are also physical needs of people in particular communities. Ultimately, I also know our enduring hope, our enduring security, our enduring life is truly found in the person of Jesus. Therefore, I want to address both physical and spiritual needs.*
>
> *I believe that we must engage these very practical physical needs while continuously pointing people back to the hope that will never fail them. Thus, my faith is a huge part of my motivation for this work. When I was doing that mini-internship, I realized the value of being involved in both realms—physical and spiritual. And I knew at that point that's what I would love to do.*

Kaleb Perdew, CLDI's current Executive Director, credits the combination of a short-term ministry experience in Kenya, a book by Bob Lupton, and the example of Jesus for propelling him into community work:

> *I visited Kenya when I was with InterVarsity as a student and spent two months living in a hut with a pastor in a village in northern Kenya. The person leading the trip reminded us that God always cares for people on the margins—such as the poor, the orphaned, and the widowed. And we learned that God has a deep concern for justice. This is not retributive justice, it's restorative justice—seeing God's heart for "the least of these" and lifting them up.*
>
> *Later I was given the book* Return Flight *by Bob Lupton, which has a chapter on empowerment.*[14] *Lupton uses the analogy of watching a butterfly struggle to get out of the cocoon. He wanted to help the butterfly and cut open the cocoon, but then the butterfly couldn't survive because it wouldn't*

have blood flow to its wings. That's when I realized that much of our helping the poor wasn't lifting them up.

Finally, I looked at the example of Jesus. Jesus was the first person that stepped down from the level he was on to the next level. Up until Jesus either someone was forcing someone else down or someone was falling, but no one stepped down voluntarily. I'm willing to live in a neighborhood that society would say represents a step down. But I've truly gained much more than I've lost from living in the South Side.

The Cost of Discipleship

Jeromy Emmerling is the Senior Pastor at First Christian Church, located in downtown Billings. Born and raised in Billings, Rev. Emmerling returned to his hometown after college to work first with a local rescue mission, then with a Christian conciliation ministry, and finally with a program on the South Side of Billings that supports at-risk families. While living with his family on the South Side, Pastor Emmerling was invited to join the staff at First Christian as associate pastor. When the former senior pastor moved on, Rev. Emmerling was appointed to the senior role.

Rev. Emmerling is deeply committed to his community and to welcoming all members of the community, including those without homes. Pastor Emmerling explains what happened when he decided to open the doors of the church to those who needed a place to rest and recuperate:

This is a church primarily composed of people who drive downtown from the suburbs. Yet we are located in a part of the city where many homeless individuals gather. There are many other churches downtown, and the typical church policy is to keep your doors locked and hope that the homeless don't sleep on your front steps. We made an intentional decision to leave our doors unlocked when we are here and to invite those folks in.

When we began to bring the homeless into our church building it created all sorts of questions and concerns. For the most part our people were ready to welcome them. We made space for conversations, such as "What do I do when someone asks me for money?" We also invited discussion about what Jesus taught regarding the poor. "What does Scripture tell us about these sorts of things?" For the most part, our people were gracious and willing to have those conversations.

> *There's an older woman who attended our church since she was born, and she had been one of those that was very critical of our decision to welcome the homeless. She came to me one day and said, "Jeromy, I was talking to my doctor, and we got to talking about church. He asked me where I went, and I told him First Christian. Then he said, "Isn't that the church that welcomes all the homeless people?" And then she said, "Pastor, I was so embarrassed!"*

First Christian's commitment to its community extends beyond welcoming the unhoused into its building. The congregation also allocates 17 percent of its annual budget to support "strategic ministry partners" like CLDI—a percentage higher than the 10 or 11 percent that most churches aspire to give to ministries beyond the congregation.[15] This elevated level of giving to local organizations has come at a cost to the maintenance of the congregation's facilities ... as has the constant presence of unhoused individuals. "Because people sleep around the building, and because things get broken, we need to replace a dozen windows a year," according to Rev. Emmerling. Pastor Emmerling also acknowledged that while some families had attended worship services at the church and "appreciated the mission and the vision and the values, they weren't comfortable exposing their kids to this space."

Despite some clear costs to the congregation, Pastor Emmerling is convinced that the benefits to the congregation of its deep engagement with the community are even more significant.

> *Community development work is the soil in which our folks are sanctified. Welcoming someone who isn't treating you well and being able to love them is a stretching thing. If you can process that experience with other folks who are supporting you, you can begin to understand what was going on. And then you can extend grace.*

The German theologian Dietrich Bonhoeffer wrote that "the church is church only when it is there for others."[16] This is demonstrated by the practice of Pastor Emmerling's congregation.

Joys and Challenges

Those who interact regularly with individuals dealing with addiction, poverty, or abuse learn to celebrate what Tabitha Kroll, the former case manager at Hannah House, calls "small victories."

For some of these women, what may seem as simple as getting a birth certificate or driver's license is a major milestone. When you watch women go from a deep hole to climbing a mountain, you see small victories that lead to significant growth.

At the same time, Kroll notes her own tendency to "want it more than they do" and then being tempted to over-function. She describes it this way:

With some of the women, you can want it so bad for them that if you're not careful, you end up trying to do it for them. We try not to do anything for them that they can do for themselves. And sometimes it's hard to know where that point is because everyone's different. It's hard to strike the balance and, since it's different with everybody, your boundaries have to vary with different people.

Internship Director Thompson reports that joy comes for her when individuals that she is accompanying develop their own faith and commit to follow Jesus. The challenges she faces resonate with Kroll's temptation to "want it more than they do."

Given what they've experienced—the hardships, the challenges—seeing them walk in hope in Jesus, against all odds, is incredible. A student that I first nurtured with the truth and the hope that's found in Jesus later did the same thing for me when I was having a difficult time. I've seen women who have experienced some of the worst that life has to offer become bearers of hope themselves.

You desperately want good things for the people that you're engaging with. You love them so much. You want life for them, but you see them making choices that you know are not going to work. If there's not the desire on their part to make the needed change, I don't have the power to change a human heart. I can offer resources or tools, and I can point someone in a direction, but I cannot change their heart. And sometimes, even when the heart changes, the habits are harder yet to change.

Along with his colleagues, Executive Director Perdew emphasizes the principle of doing "with" rather than "for" and identifies a joy as "not doing something for someone that they can do for themselves." Perdew also stresses the centrality of faith in his approach to community work. "We see the Holy Spirit change people's hearts and Jesus change people's lives, and this is so rewarding. We're creating a space for God to work." Perdew also recognizes the power imbalance that is implicit in any relationship where one party brings considerably more resources and requirements than the other:

> *I must be aware of power imbalances and know where my place is in that power dynamic. I try to be as servant-hearted as possible in assuming vulnerability along with power. If your power increases, then your vulnerability must increase in an equal measure. Generally, people with power put the vulnerability on someone else. Jesus assumed full power and full vulnerability, power and love together, which became clear on the cross. The cost of that was the ultimate vulnerable state of being naked, embarrassed, spat at, then dying – and he had the full power to avoid it.*

CLDI's philosophy stresses the importance of both relationships and resources. It seeks to draw on resources in the South Side neighborhood and in the community of Billings as a whole. Director Perdew describes this approach as follows:

> *If we aren't asset-based, if we are solely focusing on people's deficits, then all we do is put a mirror of what's wrong in front of people. This neighborhood has a heart of generosity when it's allowed to flourish and when it isn't ignored because of its deficits. We have a front porch culture in this neighborhood, where people sit in front of their homes and interact with neighbors, that I think the rest of Billings can learn from. In the South Side, we love getting to know our neighbors and having a front yard barbecue where everyone's welcome.*
>
> *I believe that there are huge benefits of history, culture, and diversity that we have in the South Side that I continue to promote in the broader community. There are needs in our neighborhood, and I'll always describe the need. But I want to start by naming the gifts that we can build on. If you tear someone down and then try and build them up, you usually just keep tearing them down.*

Framework Analysis

Reflecting on the theoretical model offered in Chapter 1, it is evident that CLDI is engaged in meeting basic human needs primarily through providing affordable housing. CLDI also effectively communicates the needs and gifts of the South Side neighborhood to the broader Billings community, thus raising awareness of injustice. However, what CLDI strives to do most is effect change in a particular neighborhood—to develop both individuals and the community they are part of.

Nevertheless, a laser focus on a particular neighborhood and on specific neighbors may risk obscuring the broader systemic issues that are driving the presenting problems. Poverty is exacerbated by the growing stratification between the rich and the poor in the US, a trend that is a direct result of public policy choices.[17] While many attribute drug addiction to a personal failing, studies suggest that pharmaceutical companies propelled the recent opioid crisis.[18] Similarly, the lack of affordable housing has been worsened by large investors who purchase homes to convert into income-producing rental units.[19]

The challenge for those focused on a particular neighborhood is thus to link their development efforts to larger regional or national organizations or movements that address systemic issues. CLDI does that through its membership in the Christian Community Development Association (CCDA), founded by Dr. John Perkins.[20] CCDA encourages its member organizations to engage in both *advocacy*, "speaking on behalf of something or someone to those in power as part of a strategy to bring systemic change," and *organizing*, "mobilizing voices around an issue that directly affects that group's community."[21]

Learnings

There are at least five lessons we can learn from Community Leadership and Development Incorporated's nearly 50 years of experience on the South Side of Billings.

1 *Movements, if they are to continue, eventually morph into formal organizations.* The movement that started with a group of young people moving into the South Side of Billings in the late 1970s and early 1980s eventually became a formal organization—CLDI. That transition was not without its challenges. The change after 30 years from a grassroots movement of young Christians to greater professionalism and staffing was "a little uncomfortable," as former executive director Eric Basye observed. However, movements that do not formalize typically tend to disappear when the founding charismatic leader departs.

2. *The process of becoming a neighbor takes years; and a landlord is not just a neighbor.* The original group of young people who moved into the South Side fifty years ago required years of residency to be perceived as genuine neighbors. Their initial contacts were with children and youth, who are often more open to building relationships with newcomers. However, as CLDI entered the business of affordable housing, the legal and financial realities of being a landlord challenged the informal and community-based aspects of simply being a neighbor.

3. *The essence of community development is leadership development.* Several key staff positions within CLDI are held by individuals who were former participants in CLDI programs. The primary focus of the Youth Works program is mentoring youth, while the internship program also focuses on leadership development. If a neighborhood is to experience economic and social development, leaders from that neighborhood need to be nurtured and developed.

4. *Faith both motivates and sustains.* Many of CLDI's employees, as well as supporting pastors in Billings, credit their Christian faith as providing the primary motivation for becoming involved in community work, encapsulated in the idea of "loving God and loving neighbor." It's also apparent that their personal faith sustains them in that work, especially when evidence of transformation seems either elusive or ephemeral. The belief that a greater power is at work empowers individuals who experience daily disappointments. This belief also helps them to trust that God is at work over the long-term, and that outcomes are not dependent on their own efforts.

5. *Community development efforts are located in a specific place.* The challenges of poverty, addiction, and lack of affordable housing that seem intractable at the national and regional levels are often amenable to interventions at the neighborhood level. As Dave Hagstrom, one of the original founders, explains, "When we focus our attention on just one neighborhood, the problems become more clear."[22]

Tim Soerens, a co-founder of the New Parish movement in the US, suggests that changes at the neighborhood level are a bulwark against the broader national trends that are inimical to community. Soerens proposes that, "As we create relationships of trust across neighborhoods, we are ... fighting against the storm of individualism and polarization that is ripping us apart."[23]

Biblical Reflection: Mark 6:7–13 and Beyond

For those in the Christian tradition, Jesus of Nazareth offers a compelling model for both leadership development and system change. Jesus created his own leadership team by calling men and women to become disciples and to follow him. Once these disciples had received both formation and training, they were sent out "two by two" to teach, heal, and learn. (Mk 6:7–13) Jesus anticipated that not every initiative would be warmly received, so he warned his disciples that some would not welcome them and would even "refuse to hear" them. (Mk 6:11)

Jesus also combined disruptive actions, such as eating with tax collectors and "sinners," with teaching and behaviors that affirmed the core teachings of Judaism. Jesus's elevation of the two greatest commandments—love for God and love for neighbor—are principles drawn directly from the Torah. (Mk 12:28–34) Jesus affirmed for his disciples that he had "not come to abolish the law or the prophets," but to fulfill them. (Mt 5:17) After his resurrection, he also interpreted his whole life and ministry through the lens of "Moses and all the prophets." (Lk 24:7) As we explored in Chapter 1, Jesus thus modeled actions for systemic change that both affirmed the life-giving aspects of his tradition inherited from Moses and challenged the religious practice of his day that ran counter to the core teachings.

Jesus called his disciples "the salt of the earth." (Mt 5:13) He also likened the coming of God's kingdom to yeast that a woman baker mixes with flour. (Mt 13:33) The art of transforming systems in a particular place can usefully be illustrated through the metaphors of salt and yeast. Salt and yeast both do their work invisibly—salt in the process of *preserving* or flavoring something that already exists, and yeast by acting as a leavening agent to *transform* the dough. Salt preserves and yeast transforms—and both are essential processes of community development. The key discernment challenge is identifying what needs to be preserved and what needs to be transformed.

CLDI serves as both salt and yeast in the South Side neighborhood of Billings, Montana. Salt, in the act of joining and maintaining the best traditions of the neighborhood, such as its "front porch culture." Yeast, in the process of the mutual transformation of people and systems in that same neighborhood. In its commitment to a specific "place," CLDI also demonstrates the most essential element of community development—that transformation always takes place in a particular context, and within a particular community.

Questions for Reflection and Group Discussion

1. Within the area that you think of as your "community," is there a particular neighborhood or portion of the community with more significant and chronic needs? What would it take to consider relocating to that neighborhood?

2. Who do you and others in your congregation know that lives or worships in that particular neighborhood or area? How have you partnered with those individuals or congregations in the past—or how could you envision doing so in future?

3. Transforming systems through community development normally requires multiple actors—including neighborhood associations, local governments, nonprofit organizations, and supportive businesses. To what extent is there any formal or informal coalition in your community? If there is none, in what ways can you and those you know imagine helping to form one?

6 Applying an Asset-Based Approach in England

An Initial Story: A Street Party

It's 9.30 a.m. on a Saturday morning in July, in one of the Firs and Bromford neighborhoods in east Birmingham, England. A white van pulls up next to a green square, about the size of a couple of tennis courts, edged on all sides by semi-detached and terraced houses, and blocks of three-level apartments. Out of the van, a man in his mid-twenties and an older woman extract a bouncy castle and a generator, which they begin setting up on the green. It's not long before another car draws up, with gazebos, bunting, a large water urn, games equipment and a giant Jenga set, among other diverse items, packed tightly around its occupants.

As the gazebos go up, the visible busyness begins to draw neighbors out of the surrounding homes, some from curiosity, but many others with a clear sense of purpose. A random collection of tables and chairs begins to assemble. No sooner are the tables set down than they become home to a quickly growing array of sandwiches, samosas and pakoras, vats of hearty rice, and cakes of all shapes and sizes.

Although this street party has been advertised to start at midday, already by 10:30 a.m. an outdoor game has self-organized, and many of the chairs are occupied by neighbors of all ages chatting—often with lots of laughter, sometimes with more serious intent or compassionate care. While several people are clearly taking on the role of welcoming new arrivals, it's not immediately obvious who, if anyone, is "running" the event. And it's quite apparent that many neighbors are meeting each other for the first time. Some adults lead arts and crafts activities with both children and other grown-ups. At one point a woman gets many of the assembled crowd on their feet, dancing a high-energy Zumba session. At peak busyness, you might be able to count around 30 children and 40 adults enjoying the party in one way or another.

It's past 5:00 p.m. by the time the buzz begins to die down. The food has mostly been eaten, the chairs and tables have disappeared with their owners back to their respective homes—but there are still enough people around to dismantle the gazebos, and to scour each square yard of the green for litter. Two boys are persuaded, reluctantly, to relinquish two bats and a ball.[1]

Approach Description

This chapter explores how Asset-Based Community Development (ABCD) has been applied and drawn upon within one parish in east Birmingham, England. ABCD is one among several strengths-based approaches developed in recent decades as alternatives to typical interventions in communities and neighborhoods facing significant perceived social deprivation and complex challenges.

Conventional work to develop strategies to alleviate poverty and inequality has focused on policies which national and local government, health and social welfare agencies, and other large institutions could take to address the perceived problems. The unstated assumption was that addressing the problems of such neighborhoods was the job of outsiders, and the focus was on tackling the deficits in those settings. Two American academics, John McKnight and Jody Kretzmann, recognized that such approaches rarely included neighbors. They undertook research into how local residents, with their inventiveness and problem-solving capacities, might become a principal party in neighborhood change. This included identifying how the range of resident people's gifts, skills and associational life—collectively designated as "assets" in their model—might be a key resource for improving the local neighborhood.[2] In 1988, McKnight and Kretzmann established the Asset-Based Community Development Institute at the Center for Urban Affairs at Northwestern University, on the outskirts of Chicago, Illinois. They went on to publish a manual setting out how to adopt an ABCD approach as an alternative, strengths-based method for achieving positive neighborhood change.[3]

ABCD has primarily been employed in a North American context—unsurprisingly given its roots. However, through the work of an Irishman, Cormac Russell, and his organization, Nurture Development, ABCD training and advocacy has been undertaken in Britain, Ireland, and elsewhere in Europe. Russell and McKnight together wrote a more recent and accessible handbook setting out the ABCD approach.[4]

In the spring of 2012, Paul Wright was a youth worker in the parish of Hodge Hill, a community in east Birmingham, England, of around 19,500 people. He spotted a two-day ABCD training course being run by Cormac Russell in West Bromwich, England, and had a hunch that it could be useful. He persuaded the rector of the parish, Al Barrett, and a new community worker, Sarah, to join him. Barrett recalls: "I remember it well because it was in Holy Week. So, as a minister I had to think carefully about saying yes. But it felt important. And, very quickly, the language that I heard on the first day was giving me some vocabulary to articulate what we'd been doing instinctively for a couple of years."[5] The three church colleagues returned to take forward a more intentional application of the ABCD approach with a focus on the Firs and Bromford neighborhoods, estates of low-income housing within their parish.[6]

However, the story of ABCD in Hodge Hill is not the story of three heroic church workers. It is a story of a relatively large-scale intervention of three grass-roots organizations: Open Door Community Foundation, a nonprofit organization formed by Hodge Hill Church, an ecumenical partnership of which Al Barrett is the rector; Worth Unlimited, a Christian-based youth work organization formed in 1997 on the back of the then newly-elected Labour government's "New Deal" initiatives to tackle the wasted human potential caused by long-term unemployment; and Firs & Bromford Neighbours Together, a community group coordinated by local residents, for local residents, which coalesced around a £1,000,000 ($1,250,000) grant to the neighborhood from the Big Local program. Big Local is a scheme run by the National Lottery Community Fund targeted at historically under-funded neighborhoods.

In 2017, these three organizations formed a partnership entitled Together We Can. This has been funded by major grants currently due to run until 2026. Together the grants to Together We Can have averaged around

£150,000 ($188,000) a year. The largest were made in two stages by the National Lottery Community Fund, in addition to the Big Local program. This funding has occurred over a strikingly long period, as anyone who has applied for grant funding will appreciate. It has thus enabled a sustained level of support activity.

The Together We Can project brings together youth work and adult-focused community-building work to maximize the opportunities for intergenerational and cross-cultural interaction and relationship-building. The project seeks to support both young people and adults on a developmental journey from first contact, through clearing obstacles and pathways into participation, towards being able to make meaningful contributions within the neighborhood and beyond. It also seeks to develop individuals' skills, confidence, and connections to initiate and lead their own groups and activities.

Key Features of Community-Building in Hodge Hill

Getting to Know the Neighborhood

Al Barrett arrived as the rector of Hodge Hill Church at an interesting time: the church had recently lost its building which had been pulled down due to major structural issues. This offered something of a blank sheet and what he saw as "a gift." Barrett and his colleagues used this situation to get to know the church's neighborhood and to learn about the place and its people more deeply.[7] Barrett said, "We wanted to see what was here. Going out and listening to the stories of our neighbors was vital to this. We wanted to hear what people loved, what their hopes and dreams were, as well as the challenges." This led to developing a community event, entitled Hodge Hill Unsung Heroes, which told stories of local people being good neighbors. The aim was to celebrate the neighborliness that they already saw in their community and to nurture and encourage it.

Timebanking: An Early Detour

Early in their development of community-building in Hodge Hill, the Open Door Community Foundation team were drawn to the possibilities of using "timebanking." Timebanking in the UK is a system where people exchange skills and time without using money, earning "time credits" for help provided to others. These credits can then be used to receive help in return.[8] It seemed to offer a sense of mutuality which was appealing, as was the exchange of practical work and the avoidance of traditional financial currency.

Despite putting some significant effort into trying to make the timebanking model work in the Firs and Bromford neighborhoods, it simply did not "take." The conclusion of Al Barrett and his colleagues was that the timebanking approach might well fit a different social and economic culture to the Hodge Hill parish context. However, in a low-income and working-class culture such as theirs, it was not a model to which local residents could readily relate.

The decision was taken to abandon trialing the timebanking approach in Hodge Hill. It felt like a detour: an avenue which had taken a significant investment of time and energy, but which did not prove fruitful in their setting. What the trial did was to cause the team to revisit how they might approach collaborative community-building. As indicated above, after a couple of years in the parish this rethinking was supported by attending an ABCD training event. The training provided a conceptual understanding and approach for Barrett and his colleagues that focused efforts on a more innovative approach to community-building in Firs and Bromford.

Community Connectors

Probably the most important inspiration from an intentional ABCD application was the approach of learning to identify and value people within the neighborhood who were naturally "community connectors," also known as "street connectors."

Paul Wright identified some of the features of a community connector: "Connectors are people who know their neighbors. They have a passion for the wellbeing of the community. They spot the gifts and goodness in other people. Connectors want to make other people feel welcome, including people on the edges and margins. They especially like to introduce and connect people with one another." What Wright observed is that community connectors are often undervalued. Partly this is because they are not obviously "leaders," in a conventional sense. Al Barrett described them as "a particular kind of gifted neighbour that knows and is known by people, is trusted, and has a particular grace, skill or art to know the person who needs help and the person that might be able to help them."

Nurturing community connectors has been at the heart of the approach in the Firs and Bromford neighborhoods. Hence Paul Wright is employed full-time in a role entitled Street Connector Mentor, which the Open Door Community Foundation invented. In the first instance, Wright's role involved identifying people who are natural community connectors and looking to affirm their gift. Over time, the role has involved regularly bringing together a team of street connectors to help them reflect on what they are doing and what is going on in the neighborhood. This has included supporting the community connectors as they go out and knock on people's doors as well as helping them identify opportunities for involvement in community conversations.

Wright told this story to illustrate how a community or street connector can work:

> *I remember this one guy, Jim, who came to a street party. One of our street connectors, Penny, came darting up to me saying, "Where's Phil? Because I've found a guy called Jim, and he's just come back to look after his sister, from working at a holiday camp. He's got time on his hands. He used to be a stage manager, and he's up for joining in." So, we found Phil, who heads up the theater group, and connected them together. Then at the next pantomime, Jim's in charge of backstage.*
>
> *But I found out two years later, the funniest thing was that Jim hadn't even intended coming to the street party. He'd popped down the shop, noticed the street party, wandered over and started chatting. Obviously, he started chatting with Penny. And before he knows it, he's been collared and is part of the theater group.*

This was a story of a passer-by who was drawn into the community story unintentionally. It certainly was not what Jim had been expecting when going to the local shop. However, through a conversation with a street connector, who knew how to ask suitable questions, his stage-managing skills were illuminated. A connection was then made with the community theater group, in need of those very skills. Paul later contrasted this with some of the more intentional conversations that community connectors have with their neighbors.

Bumping Spaces

A second vital ingredient of community-building in Hodge Hill has been identifying what they call "bumping spaces." These may be a "gift of the physical environment" or just spaces with significant human interaction, where people can metaphorically bump into one another. Having identified these spaces, those involved in community-building have then been intentional about finding ways to "hang out" in them.

Barrett, Wright, and their colleagues noticed that there were few such bumping spaces on the Firs and Bromford estates. So, they have taken the initiative to create some. One was created through becoming part of a national network called Places of Welcome.[9] The Open Door Community Foundation's local Place of Welcome is held one morning a week at a local rented shop front. During the advertised hours, people from the community can drop in for a hot drink and a conversation. Wright named this shop front The Hub, to reflect the desire for it to be a place of encounter for local neighbors. Barrett noted that,

> *It's quite consciously different to an advice center where you come with a need, have it met, and go away again. Rather, it's a space where, if you come, we expect you to fall in love with it and to want to come next week—just because you've made friends and want to hang out. If, in the process, you get some needs met, that's great. But it becomes a bumping space, a center of community.*

One way that this sense of community is nurtured is through encouraging participation in making a cup of tea. Paul Wright commented that,

> *We try not to have a situation where people are serving tea. If someone would like a cup of tea, we may well say, "Help yourself—and why don't you ask if anyone else wants one?" Most people can make a cup of tea or can be taught to make one quite quickly. That's something that they can offer as a simple gift to others.*

Through encouraging such participation, people are given a greater sense of agency and a way of contributing to community life.

Another example of a bumping space has been a "pop-up" one, which involved setting up a table serving hot drinks outside the gate of one of the local schools. This has provided an opportunity for conversations with parents and carers of school children when they are dropping off or picking up their child. It has also helped parents and carers to get into conversation with one another. Al Barrett noticed that, "There's a whole different conversation that happens when you're hanging out with other parents at the school gates than there is when those same people are in a church space, for example." He saw being present in spaces that the church did not own or run to be part of shifting the power balance in the church's relationships in the local community, empowering their neighbors more.

Street Parties and Scale

One of the Open Door Community Foundation's community-building efforts has focused on supporting neighbors to hold relatively small-scale street parties, mostly during the summer months. The aim is for these to be neighbor-led. Paul Wright gave one illustration of this:

> *A wonderful example was the recent Eid party. We've had street parties for some time now which are becoming part of the local culture. To help run a street party, there's a small fund people can apply to. In our street, one party was held to mark the Queen's Diamond Jubilee; and another for the coronation of King Charles. Then one of our Muslim neighbors asked, "Can we have an Eid al-Adha party?" So that happened to mark a major Muslim festival: they ran the whole event and invited us all—just as we'd invited them all to our Christmas carol singing on the street. For the Eid party, we handed the organization over and just said, "Let us know what you want us to do." It was a great example of handing over to someone else and not being the church always running things* for *people.*

Al Barrett emphasized how these street events and parties were designed to support neighbors to be connectors in their own street, square, or cul-de-sac:

> *We are encouraging neighbors to be hosts in a place that doesn't particularly have a culture of inviting people around to dinner but does have a growing culture of street parties. Where neighbors will knock on each other's doors and say, "Can you bring some tables and chairs? Can you bring some cakes? What about the drink? And can you bring the games?" And it's held on the*

communal green, or on the street. So, these street parties are another kind of bumping space, a more temporary one.

In our evaluation work, we've discovered that when a big event is put on in the community and the people come in family groups and consume, they'll have a lovely day. But when we ask them, "At the end of the day, how many of your neighbors have you got to know by name today?", most people will say none. Whereas, in a little street event, about 80 percent of people who come will say they've gotten to know several neighbors by name for the first time. That's weaving a fabric of neighborliness and connectedness. So, we've found that promoting smaller scale things really facilitates people getting to know one another. It also empowers people to be participants in helping and enabling the event to actually happen.

Smallness is therefore an important principle in all of this. It's not something you can upscale; although it is something that you can proliferate. So, part of our work is to encourage more street parties to happen in different parts of the neighborhood with different hosts. We're not aiming to make one street party bigger and bigger, so that eventually the whole neighborhood comes to it—because that loses the key ingredients.

Neighbor-led Activities

In addition to street parties, other neighbor-led activities have included "Mindful Walks," which a community member, Nicola, started during the Covid pandemic. Nicola instigated, organizes, and runs these reflective walks for people in the neighborhood, with Paul Wright providing some support.

A similar type of initiative came from another community member, Soobie, who said that she would like to run a dance group. Open Door Community Foundation and their partners were able to support this through finding a suitable space and organizing safeguarding checks. However, as the independent evaluator, Jane Perry commented, "The passion, the leadership, and all of the volunteer energy that it takes to run that dance group comes from community members rather than from any paid staff."

One feature that Paul Wright observed is how their community-builders can be highly responsive when someone in the community has an idea that they would like to take forward. He illustrated the point through this story:

We were just coming out of Covid restrictions. The flood defenses were being built along the river Tame next to us. As part of that, they'd dug up the only playground on the estate and didn't replace it as soon as hoped. Linda, a community member, said, "But it's the school holidays. The children need somewhere to play. Not everybody can afford to travel to a playground elsewhere." So, Linda came over to The Hub and said, "I want to run a little playground for mothers and toddlers. I've got children and grandchildren, so I've got toys, equipment, and soft mats."

We were outside. A few others pulled up chairs and we sat in a circle. Within half an hour we'd planned it all out. Linda was going to do this. Clare would bring face paints. Someone else would bring another resource. We'd contribute some gazebos and maybe source a bouncy castle. We'd do it three afternoons a week and I'd open The Hub. It just emerged, all those gifts and skills. Then it was done. I remember that we had a placement student with us whose jaw dropped. She asked, "Have I just experienced ABCD?" What astonished her was that it just happened. We didn't arrange a meeting in two weeks' time to plan it.

Engaging with Negative Energy

As a street connector, Penny Hall also spoke about the need for connectors to engage with negative energy during their street connecting. She offered this example:

We visited some of the smaller apartment blocks and knocked door-to-door saying, "Hello, we're your local neighbors. How are you?" One person made a complaint: "We can't even play outside in the communal garden." This was because it didn't appear to be anyone's responsibility to keep the grass cut. I responded, "With a little bit of support, if you had the tools, if you could borrow a lawnmower, could you see yourself doing anything?" We were aware that there were a few positive people in those apartments, including some would-be gardeners: people who could be creative with a bit of support. But it needed the people who lived there to get engaged. So, we asked for their ideas, "What would you like to see in your garden?" And then, "Well, why not?" One of the neighbors mentioned, "I know somebody that's got loads of flowers: let's ask if we can have cuttings from them." So, that's how they developed their garden area, after they'd borrowed a lawnmower.

She noted that she did not get directly involved herself. Instead, she asked questions (as a coach might do) which built on the energy in the initial negative complaint, prompting people to take action for themselves. This process of helping to empower local people has been at the heart of the community-building process in Hodge Hill: enabling local people to take responsibility for action and taking something forward.

From Supported to Neighbor-led Activities

Sometimes activities are initially supported by paid staff, before becoming more neighbor-led. Jane Perry, the independent evaluator, offered this example:

> *Ambridge House is a collection of supported housing that's in-between the main tower blocks on the estates and that has its own social space. Flo and Dan, two of the youth workers supported by Worth Unlimited, organized the young people to put on a tea party for the older people as a youth social action project. So, the idea was started by the youth workers. However, over time some of the young people and some of the older ones liked the gatherings so much that they started asking to do it again. The request became neighbor-led. The youth workers increasingly stepped back. Now the Ambridge teas are led by two adult community members. They and the young people get on with hosting these intergenerational tea parties pretty much on their own. That in turn led on to some intergenerational games: some of the old people taught the younger ones how to play bingo.[10] They found it fun. Now they host bingo sessions that are intergenerational, as part of enjoying being together.*

Development of Individuals

Alongside this empowerment of groups within the neighborhood, the team have documented a gradual journey in the development of individuals. People are initially drawn in as participants in a particular activity. Then they are invited to become volunteers. Some of them are then encouraged to take on leadership. Jane Perry emphasized that this is not a straightforward or linear process. Instead, the community-building team conceives of this as more of a spiral. Nevertheless, embedded in the project is what she observed as: "that idea of developing and empowering people. Giving them training and experience, where that's needed. And supporting them to be able to move on to do more than they'd expected."

The Local Church and Theological Articulation

Several of the volunteers and most of the paid staff involved in the community-building project are part of the church; and establishing the Open Door Community Foundation was a church initiative. The primary focus of this Foundation is the two most challenging neighborhoods located within the parish, Firs and Bromford. However, the church building is located slightly away from these neighborhoods. Therefore, a significant decision for the church congregation was to host a pantry, part of the Your Local Pantry network, within their church building.[11] For a small weekly subscription—£4 ($5) at time of writing—members of the Hodge Hill Pantry can purchase a weekly food shop including fresh fruit and vegetables and family favorites for the cupboard. Therefore, unlike a food bank, the produce is not given away; rather subscribers pay for their goods, which helps their self-respect and sense of ownership. People from Open Door and Hodge Hill Church host and run this pantry together—and pantry subscribers are encouraged to get involved as volunteers. Alongside the pantry, the church hosts a weekly café serving food and drink. Penny Hall, as both a church member and a street connector, has noticed how this hosting has been important for both church members and their neighbors:

> People in the church really got involved, probably because it was in our building. They really enjoyed it, engaging with the neighbors and contributing to the café catering. In the process, suddenly there's no distinction between the people who're church members and the people who've come up from the estate to use the pantry and who are encouraged to be the volunteers to enable it all to happen and to set everything out.
>
> My next-door neighbor, who doesn't go to church, comes and sets up the day before the pantry operates. She sets out all the food in readiness, stacks the shelves with stuff that's come in and helps set out the furniture. If we get huge bags of rice, she'll weigh it out into family-sized bags. So, she engages and is a hugely important part of the pantry. But she doesn't go to church. Equally, there are others who go to church that also get involved in the pantry. Through this, the social barrier between church and the estate has become blurred.

There's a sense of, "We're in this together, we're equal partners here." There isn't a dynamic of, "We're church, and you're neighborhood."

Paul Wright observed that this had contributed to a sense that, "the church building is a space that's a community space as well." There is a more mutual sense of ownership of the church space and of the church being *of* the community. The boundaries between the church and her neighbors are being broken down.

The rector of the parish, Al Barrett, saw this as contributing to a notable change within the church:

There's also been a real shift in how many members of the church will talk about the kingdom of God. I've found it moving to observe the number of congregation members who now have tangible experienced examples, lived stories to tell that are the equivalent of Jesus's parables of the kingdom. It's no longer abstract language.

The great Ann Morisy once made the distinction between proclaimed hope and enacted hope.[12] Often the church will tell people that they should be hopeful, because there are reasons for their hope. Whereas enacted hope is about actually living it, and people experiencing a hopeful world, a hopeful environment, a hopeful community; and then being able to articulate that hope out of their experience.

Among my neighbors, and also among my church community, we've been more in the business of enacted hope than proclaimed hope. And that has changed the way people talk and proclaim, out the other end. They can say, "Look, there's the kingdom of God; it feels like this; and it tastes like that."

Challenges and Issues Faced with Community-Building

Paying Community Connectors and Engaging the Employed

Those interviewed were realistic about some of the issues and challenges that they have faced. Jane Perry observed this in relation to paying some of the community connectors:

> *There's an interesting tension around paid work. In simplistic ABCD talk it's easy to make it sound like: if somebody's being paid to do something then it's no longer neighbor-led. One pushback we've offered is to say that sometimes things do need to be paid. This then raises the question, "What does it mean to be a neighbor who is paid to do something? And what does it mean for the project for the neighbor-led thing to have a paid element?" We're still exploring what it means for paid staff to hold that kind of dual role. There are huge benefits but also real issues. Obviously, without infinite funding, you can't bring all your neighbors into paid employment: that's not realistic.*

ABCD holds that neighbors are often best placed to do things for themselves. In practice, some activities either need paid time or professional expertise. In addition, a person in a paid role can come alongside groups or individuals who would be leading things anyway, and, with some light support, can enable those things to happen more confidently and competently.

A related challenge was identified by Paul Wright, who observed how difficult it was to engage those already in paid employment: "To be able to do all this community-building, you need *time*. So, we've always struggled to engage the people who are working. We have some. But many of our people are either retired or unemployed: they might be long-term sick or off work. However, with us they find ways to contribute to the neighborhood."

Individual and Community Level Impact

In exploring the impact of community-building, evaluator Jane Perry recognized that this needs to be assessed at both an individual and a community level:

> *The theory of change for the whole Together We Can project explicitly attempts to hold together individual human development with community development. So, the overall aim is: "Developing our community into a place of creativity and compassion where all feel welcome, all feel connected, all feel they belong, and all feel they can flourish," which tends to get summarized as "a flourishing community." The theory of change identifies community outcomes, of what the community would need to look like if this was happening; but also, what you'd expect to see in the lives of individuals if this was happening. One of the challenges, but also one of the joys, is holding together the community and individual elements.*

The flourishing of both individuals and communities are mutually interlinked: you can't concentrate on just one or the other, you've got to find a way of holding both in tandem. That's significant, because many projects would just focus on individual self-fulfillment, growth, or flourishing. Whereas Together We Can attempts to hold both together.

Envisaging Growth

Linked to the question of flourishing is how growth is envisaged within the project. Perry went on to name the issue in this way:

Although we do count things, there's an acute awareness that more and more activity is not in itself a good thing. Rather, it's the overall blossoming of activity, whether or not things last, which is the sign of a healthy community. Not that more people are doing more and more; or, even worse, fewer people doing more and more. This challenges the cultural norm that "more" is necessarily an indicator of success. Yes, you want to see more neighbors getting involved, and you want to see more spaces for people to connect. However, only within the limits of both the local context and the lifecycle of things.

Leadership

Another challenge is around the question of leadership—although how leadership is framed is not necessarily straightforward. Paul Wright helpfully articulated the issue:

It is crucial to have leadership. Even saying this I'm cringing; because it's not a top-down thing. But having leadership, whatever word you want to describe it, is so important. This stuff doesn't just happen. That leadership comes from lots of places in our story here, not just Al Barrett, the rector, who has certainly been key. There's a whole community outside of the church where leadership has happened, and this work has been taken forward. Every word I use, I question. Is it oversight? I don't like the word. But it needs people to be guiding, nurturing, supporting, and encouraging.

Al Barrett does a huge amount, but there are many other people involved in leadership, inside and outside the church. The big question is, "When Al leaves, what's still going?" That will be evidence of how much has become embedded. There's a culture shift that has happened here that will live on – both in this neighborhood and in the church. Even if individual things end, there's a culture that has changed here that will continue in different shapes and forms. And the role of gentle, holding leadership or oversight, will remain crucial.

The diversification of leadership, with this being spread across a range of individuals, is likely to be a key indicator of strength within the network of community-building in Hodge Hill. As Wright identified, this will also increase the chances of sustainability over time, when one key leader eventually moves on.

Limitations of ABCD

Mental Health Challenges

Given the length of time of the community-building project in Hodge Hill, it is not surprising that the team involved have encountered some of the limitations of the ABCD approach. One of these is addressing people's mental health challenges, as described here by Al Barrett:

> *Our neighbors talk about mental health struggles as being a particular challenge for many of us. Covid exacerbated that and exposed it more sharply. We are passionate believers in the peer support of neighbors, spaces of belonging and of encounter, conversation and friendship being vital to sustaining and nurturing people's positive mental health. At the same time, we acknowledge those don't do everything; sometimes what people really need is a professional counsellor to talk to; or professional mental health support to access psychiatry and medication.*
>
> *So, we're working on identifying the capacity within our community to support people's mental health, in terms of people that have lived experience, including navigating professional services, and that are up for sharing experience and journeying with others as they access such services. We are therefore looking for more robust forms of signposting and advocacy in helping people access professional services. We've realized these need to be part of the picture. What ABCD does is ask, "Where do you start?" ABCD challenges the ingrained assumption that you start with professional help. ABCD says, "Let's start with community. Let's see what community can do." And our community here has some amazing grassroots ways of supporting people's mental health; but, at the same time, it's not the whole picture and can't cover everything.*

The range of groups and activities mentioned earlier in the chapter all contribute to this mental health support.

Structures and Personality Tensions

Barrett also identified the value of some organizational structure and paid staff in addressing limitations of the ABCD approach, for example in dealing with tensions and frictions between different personalities.

> *I've learnt the hard way, over 13 years here, that sometimes structures are important to be able to do some of the work that relationships without structure are less good at doing. That's often about the way different personalities can rub up against each other; and sometimes create more heat than light. The structure can offer some protection for activities that might otherwise have fallen victim to personality clashes. Our instinct has been to be light on structure. But sometimes our desire to run with people's passions means that one person's passion has wounded others. Or the flame of passion has burned brightly and then burnt out, leaving others disappointed. Part of the gift of some paid staff has been to offer stability and continuity that has enabled some things that have been more neighbor-led to burn and then fizzle out because that's been part of the life cycle.*

Individuals' Fragilities

Related to this has been the challenge of working with the fragilities of individuals' lives, as Barrett went on to explain:

> *Amidst this are the fragilities of people in a low-income neighborhood like ours with multiple physical, health, and livelihood challenges. Some people were right at the center of leading things. Then something happened that's knocked them for six. Paid staff and some organizational structures have offered a safety net to catch some of that: work that feels vital to sustain, alongside the other stuff that is okay to let go of. That's been hard.*

This was echoed in some observations by Paul Wright:

> *We've lost half of our street connecting team either because they've struggled with their mental health and stepped away, or because they've had to find paid work. How can people sustain engagement and involvement, through*

the ups and downs of life? People can end up carrying a fair bit and that takes its toll. The fact that people are given a chance to have responsibility and take on leadership and roles—people who've never been asked before—is life-giving. It's empowering them, which is wonderful. But it also comes with stresses, worries, and anxieties. The beauty of it can also be one of the problems: it's double-edged.

Where people are not in paid employment, they can be subject to a range of vulnerabilities. They may be older or have poorer health. They are more likely to have caring responsibilities, either for children or for people who are ill. As Jane Perry observed:

Many of the people who've got most time to give can also be most subject to the kinds of vulnerabilities which mean that they're either less reliable, or struggling to contribute alongside other commitments. Burnout is therefore something that hovers on the horizon for both paid staff and volunteers. That's not unique to ABCD projects but it's a challenge to some of the rhetoric. How do you keep that sustainable for individuals and for groups?

Growth and Territoriality

Barrett went on to identify a couple of further challenges, following growth in the community-building work over time and when some neighbors have been territorial:

Thinking of the neighborhood as a whole community ecology, for a period, one or more of us could have an overview of what was going on and could attend when something needed attention. However, things have now grown to a level of complexity where that's no longer possible. So, the ecology, the organism has had to be more decentralized. Which puts extra weight on lines of communication and connection between different elements. If some of those aren't working well, then things can go a bit awry.

We've also been intentional about trying to resist territoriality as much as possible. But others within the neighborhood, that haven't necessarily bought into our way of doing things, have sometimes held on to a territorial mindset. They've then either been resentful that they're not part of something bigger, because they've not understood our focus on making connections. Or, they've been competitive and defensive around boundaries saying, "This is ours." That has been hard for us.

> *We face a dilemma. We want to be hugely attentive to power imbalances; to resist being the expert; to resist bringing answers. But nevertheless, being almost evangelistic about a particular way of doing things; and wanting people to catch that, knowing that we can't force that on them; and we can feel frustrated when some don't get it.*

ABCD as a Spectrum

In her evaluative work in Hodge Hill, Jane Perry noted that there is a risk of being too simplistic in trying to apply an ABCD approach. She saw the questions asked with an ABCD lens as being at the heart of what is useful:

> *Where ABCD does have real value is in shaping the questions that one asks: "How can we be more neighbor-led? How can we be more participative?" And in providing that checking question, "Hold on a minute, are we doing this because we think it would be good for people? Or are we doing it because they've actually asked? Are we doing this because we've always done it? Or are we doing it because there's energy from the community?" That's where ABCD is most useful.*

This has led Perry to focus less on whether a project fulfils some notion of pure ABCD criteria, "Is this ABCD?", and instead to observe that there is a continuum or spectrum: "You can be more or less asset-based; and you can be more neighbor-led or less. It's not a binary choice."

Community Ecology and Death

Al Barrett also spoke about the limitations of the ABCD model as he has developed his thinking around the idea of a community ecology:

> *By community ecology, I mean treating a neighborhood as a whole—all the moving and static parts within it—and less as a machine and more as a living ecology. So, things will grow and then tail off and die. But all are part of the ecology, and in reality are dependent on each other in some form; but often they aren't necessarily aware of that. So, encouraging that sense of intentional interdependence within the community means that, among other things, there's a certain amount of superfluity or redundancy within it. Things can flourish and die and that's okay, because we're not just dependent on that bit of the ecology for the whole thing to survive.*

> *A recent insight here is that even a dead tree contributes nutrients to the ongoing ecosystem. Therefore, being conscious of the gifts of decay and death is part of what's needed. I'm cautious about the easy language within ABCD of using what's strong and just focusing on strengths. Because there can be profound gifts in vulnerability and weakness, and in decay and death, that are just as nourishing for the community ecosystem as the things that look strong.*
>
> *The ABCD language and frameworks are helpful, up to a point. However, even the language of assets is problematic because it places things within an economic understanding, whereas the language of gift gives us a much richer theological understanding. Gifts are not to be accumulated in the ways assets are often understood to be. Gifts can change and evolve. Gifts can be fragile. Gifts can be wounds and vulnerabilities.*

Theologically, this seems an important insight that Barrett names here.[13] For God's love and purposes are often revealed through weakness, brokenness, and death, which can then become gifts to the wider world.

Framework Assessment

In reflecting on the impact of the community-building work that has been undertaken over more than a decade, Al Barrett offered this reflection:

> *I'm most heartened by the fact that all around me, people are telling a different kind of story to the one that was being told when we arrived 13 years ago. Then, a lot of people would say, "Bromford is a rubbish place to live. Nothing happens here, I can't wait to get out. We have no idea why you'd want to come and live on an estate like this." And in the church, people were saying, "We have no idea why you'd want to come and be our pastor."*
>
> *I don't want to paint it as a rags-to-riches kind of picture. But now there are many more stories being told about the riches of this community, what happens here, and the sense of community spirit enabling this. There are stories of people actively choosing to come back and live here, or to come and live here for the first time, because of what this community has now got. There's a sense that we have a good story to tell here; and the church is part of that story. And that's part of God's story, part of the kingdom of God. We see it, feel it, and live it in the profoundly local.*

There is a newly found pride. The kind of pride that is both a celebration of what's been historically marginalized, and a bit of protest, of saying, "No, we're not going to take it. We're going to be out and proud in us." There's a fair bit of that in the stories of these communities. Rather than a restoration, I see it as a discovery for the first time, of something new and that comes from God's future.

Something's also shifted with the idea of a community ecology. We've begun to name the Eucharistic table as one table among many in our community: we've discovered the joy of feasting around some of those other tables. At the same time, there's also a sense that feasting around the Eucharistic table is something holy, wonderful, special, joyful, abundant, and of God—and wouldn't it be lovely if some of the neighbors that we've met along the way discovered that alongside us, as well?

It's been much less about looking around and counting the numbers, and celebrating when the numbers go up, and feeling anxious when the numbers go down. There's something wonderful in Jesus's parables that's resonant with this, about when one person who has been coming to Open Door for ages finds their way to church one Sunday, and feels a welcome, and shares in some form—then there's a rejoicing in that.

There's something profoundly eschatological about this community-building stuff. It's a glimpse of the coming kingdom. It's a foretaste of the heavenly banquet. While there's a little bit of space for nostalgia, it's mostly about discovering something that's still emerging.

Barrett explicitly articulates something of the journey towards experiencing a foretaste of the life of heaven here on earth. This has emerged through the increased connectedness that has been fostered, building on an ABCD approach, and going beyond it. This also resonates with the journey of the two foundational Biblical stories explored in Chapter 1.

At the same time, Barrett and his colleagues are mindful of the limitations of their community-building work to address some of the structural and systemic issues faced by people in their neighborhood. This was most clearly expressed by Paul Wright:

We've started to think more about some of the systemic issues. There's some serious structural inequality in this community. There is so much poverty, with low quality housing: people having to put up with poor living conditions and rogue landlords. We can give one-to-one support and offer them community life. Those are important. But are we going, "It's not good enough that people have to live in moldy housing blocks, and their kids have got asthma as a result." Those more systemic things are not necessarily getting tackled. And the question is, "How do you do that, anyway?" Community-building takes so much time, energy, and care. It's tiring and can be draining. How do we have the time and energy to deal with the bigger stuff?

We're not ignoring it. We've got a good relationship with our Member of Parliament who values what we do. If one of our team emails him, he does respond, knowing that it must be something serious. And we are now looking at community organizing. A few of us have joined a community union. Do we need to explore more of a campaigning approach? If we're doing community-building and not doing the campaigning, are we papering over the cracks? Not intentionally. But maybe we just haven't got the time, the energy, or the mechanisms.

The two approaches can go hand-in-hand. One of our street connectors, Penny, has been talking about it for years. She's done community-organizing with Citizens UK and is a big believer in trade union type approaches. The collective effort for change that the union-type and community-organizing approach addresses can be missing within our ABCD-type community-building, through limitations on our time and capacity.

Community-building addresses a fundamental need for connection and neighborliness amongst people within a local community. As part of this work, those involved certainly become aware of issues of inequality and injustice in their community. What Wright acknowledges is that the journey towards a greater taste of heaven on earth also requires ways of challenging the system and making structural change, as highlighted by the Reconciling Mission theoretical model in Chapter 2. Community-organizing is one way of trying to achieve that, beyond what community-building can accomplish.[14]

Also implied within Wright's comments is the recognition that some people will feel more called and energized by engaging in community-building activity, while others will feel more called and committed to community-organizing work. Both need the other if they are to be part of bringing lasting and effective change within a neighborhood, to evidence more of God's purposes for humankind and to embody more fully the Together We Can vision of a flourishing community.

Biblical Reflection: The Feeding of 5,000+

All four gospel writers offer an account of the miraculous feeding of 5,000 men—the only ones who would traditionally be counted—presumably along with many thousands of women and children.[15] While there are limitations in connecting this story with community-building in Hodge Hill, the local church has found it deeply resonant for their situation. This is both because so much of their community life centers around meals—including outdoors—and because it captures some of the messy, organic nature of their work.[16]

There are some common threads to the Biblical narrative, which we can note from Mark's account. The disciples are overwhelmed by the need to feed such a huge mass of people in testing circumstances: "This is a deserted place, and the hour is now very late," (Mk 6:35) following on from a hectic period where they themselves "had no leisure even to eat." (Mk 6:31) They are acutely aware of their own lack of resources to meet the crowd's need, asking whether Jesus expects them to go and spend more than half a year's salary on buying bread for everyone. Hence, they urge Jesus to "send [the people] away so that they may go into the surrounding country and villages and buy something for themselves to eat." (Mk 6:36) At one level, this is not an unreasonable expectation: that these people should take responsibility for looking after themselves.

The early disciples reflect the anxiety experienced by many of today's churches in the UK and the USA who are aware of their dwindling numbers, resources, and capabilities; and who may be hoping that people will be self-sufficient, as our culture often expects, or alternatively that someone else will find a way to meet the needs within their local community. To the early disciples, Jesus says: "How many loaves have you? Go and see." In ABCD terms, today's churches might translate this as a challenge to focus on what we have got, rather than what we are lacking: to identify our current gifts, strengths and passions, rather than bewail our deficits.

In John's account, it is striking that the loaves and fish which are found by the disciples come from "a boy" in the crowd. (Jn 6:9) This can be a prompter that the gifts, skills and treasures which the church should be seeking are as likely (or more so?) to be found within the wider community as among the Christian community itself—including among those at the margins, such as young people, whom we might not necessarily expect to turn to.

The four gospel accounts agree that Jesus "looked up to heaven, and blessed and broke the loaves, and gave them to his disciples to set before the people," and did likewise with the two fish. (Mk 6:41) This suggests that today there could be a role for our churches to play in blessing what we find, whether through affirming, connecting, enhancing, or simply naming the gifts offered by others, if we are called to emulate Jesus in some measure.

Among the surprises of the gospel story is that there is enough and more to go around. The huge crowd of people, "all ate and were filled; and [the disciples] took up twelve baskets full of broken pieces and of the fish." (Mk 6:41) This is something of the testimony of the community-building work in Hodge Hill: despite major social needs within their community, a partnership of local people and organizations—including the local church and many church members—has enabled them together to find that they have more than enough to share with one another in being good neighbors, and in weaving a web of neighborliness—a true "foretaste of the heavenly banquet."

Questions for Reflection and Group Discussion

1 As you have read this chapter, which aspects of the community-building approach are you most intrigued by, and why is that?

2 In what ways might your local church's missional engagement take some inspiration from the stories and approach offered here? How might you follow up on this?

3 To what extent do you consider that your local congregation(s) is finding ways to address the systemic or structural issues negatively affecting people in your community? What might a further and better organized step look like?

7 Concluding Threads

In this concluding chapter we distill insights and threads from across the preceding chapters, note commonalities and distinctives, and identify what is useful about the Reconciling Mission framework. We also explore something of what sustains people on the missional journey on which the Holy Spirit calls the people of God to embark.

The flow of the following distillations reflects a classic route taken by congregations and parishes in their engagement with local communities. First, the Christian community seeks to know and love the place where we find ourselves. Next, we form deeper relationships with our neighbors. We then try to build coalitions with other groups and organizations, and to identify and develop those with leadership capabilities. It is often only then that a gathered congregation sees the need to address more systemic issues. Throughout this journey, the Christian community seeks to depend patiently on God. Although this is the final identified thread, it will be woven throughout the others if God's people are to be led by the Spirit, rather than the latest trends.

Focusing on a Particular Place

Recently we have seen renewed attention to the local neighborhood as a focus of attention and an arena for action.[1] While not a surprise, this was affirmed throughout this book's various case studies. John McKnight, co-founder of the Asset-Based Community Development Institute, observed that what people feel is their "neighborhood" tells you what they are motivated to do something about. The motivation for people to act is closely tied to a place to which they have a sense of belonging, and which they feel is theirs. Therefore, if we want to organize to change or improve a local community, we must depend on people's sense of identity with a place, because that is where their commitment is rooted.[2]

Tim Soerens and his colleagues in the New Parish Movement offer a working definition of "parish" as "a geographic area that is large enough to live life together (live, work, play, etc.) and small enough to be known as a character within it."[3] They recognize that this will look different between an urban context, where it might comprise a single neighborhood; a suburban context, where it might be the entire subdivision; and, a rural context, which might cover a much larger physical area.[4]

For those working within a traditional parish model, such as parishes within the Church of England, this can produce tension. Local people's sense of "their" neighborhood may not map onto historic parish boundaries, whereas worshipping members of the church may feel a particular parish allegiance. Depending on the context and size of the parish, this is likely to place a priority on neighboring churches working collaboratively together across parish lines. Differing theological traditions across the parishes will make this more challenging.

Sometimes, as in Hodge Hill, in Birmingham, England, there may be a choice to focus on a smaller neighborhood than the whole parish. Smaller can be not just more beautiful, but more effective. One reason is that a relational web is more realistic and more achievable on a smaller scale. In Hodge Hill they have focused some of their energies on local street parties for a single street or group of houses. Residents have found that at the end of such a gathering, people are likely to know their neighbors by name, more than is possible with a larger scale event.

Tim Soerens observed that, "We need a place to listen and learn. We need a place where we can feel the effects of our actions and make creative iterations. We need a place where we can pursue the dreams of God within our common life."[5] Our local neighborhoods offer the prospect for such a place, in a way that larger scale areas do not. A group of congregations that fully know their local neighborhood and that build strong relationships with their neighbors offer the prospect of realizing more of God's reign in their locality in partnership with those neighbors.

In Chapter 2, the parish churches of Berkswich and of St Anne's, Chasetown, illustrate this among the many examples from parishes whose clergy have participated in the Reconciling Mission program. The ecumenical parish of Hodge Hill demonstrates this in a challenging urban context.

In Billings, Montana, Community Leadership and Development Inc. (CLDI) remains keenly focused since its founding on the South Side neighborhood. All program sites, including Hannah House and the Rail//Line Coffee Shop, are located within the South Side neighborhood, and the CLDI headquarters building lies at the northern edge of that neighborhood. Most importantly, as noted earlier, more than half of CLDI employees live in the South Side.

Place matters. We belong to a defined place. We identify with a particular place. We feel motivated to act and to build relationships in that specific place. When a congregation chooses to engage with its local community, it starts by naming and understanding where it has been placed. Place then becomes both the locus of its life together and the shaper of its work.

At the same time, we recognize that local congregations embody multiple functions—an internal commitment to worship, discipleship, and fellowship along with an external focus on mission and service. Along with engaging in its place and local community, every healthy congregation must therefore also attend to the formation and integration of its own members and to corporate worship. The sociologist of religion Nancy Tatom Ammerman expresses this well, "Congregations are both sacred places, making claims for the power of a transcendent Other in the midst of this world, and civic places, mobilizing all sorts of resources for the sake of the community."[6] Enabling a congregation to strike the right balance is part of the art of ordained ministry today.[7]

Forming Respectful Relationships

Tim Soerens succinctly expresses a second thread which ties together the various case studies explored in this book:

> *We don't need to be afraid of our neighbors; we need to learn from them. Christians do not have the market cornered on being kind, generous, or loving. The fruits of the Spirit are on display in all sorts of people.*[8]

A vital starting point is recognizing that God has given our neighbors gifts, skills, and passions which are of God. We in the Christian church can therefore both learn from and connect with our neighbors. As Christians, it means we start with the assumption that there is treasure to be discovered among our neighbors who do not share our faith, rather than assuming we have the answers that our neighbors need.[9] This does not mean hiding our love of Jesus and commitment to follow him. Rather it means we maintain a commitment to building mutually respectful relationships with our neighbors, undergirded by the conviction that we have much to learn from one another.

For many of us in the church this may require greater humility than we have shown in the past. A humility which the church may say that she aspires to, but which her strategizing suggests she struggles to live out.[10] This means that we are looking to connect with the humanity that we share with our neighbors and to build genuine and long-lasting relationships—rather than seeing these relations as serving a transactional purpose or about filling our empty pews.

We may rightly long for our neighbors to discover their own relationship with God through Jesus. However, we do not make our relationship conditional on them taking that road. Rather we seek to emulate the unconditional love of God, as Jesus teaches his disciples (see Mt 5:43–48). This means being mindful that, "The truth is that we likely have more to learn from [our neighbors] than we have to teach."[11]

The centrality of such mutually respectful relationships is seen throughout the case studies offered in this book. For example, the staff and volunteers of Community Leadership and Development Inc. (CLDI) in Billings, Montana have demonstrated a passion to form respectful relationships for nearly 50 years. It began with a decision by young Christians to move into the South Side of Billings, a neighborhood widely perceived as high in both poverty and crime. And it continued through the programs that emerged from the felt needs of the community—for healthy food, youth development, addiction recovery, and affordable housing. The many staff of CLDI resident in the South Side neighborhood reveal an ongoing commitment to form mutually respectful relationships. Similarly, the community-building project in east Birmingham, England, that Hodge Hill Church has been part of over the course of the last 13 years, is wholly grounded in establishing such relationships.

Building Organizational Coalitions

A third striking thread running through this book's case studies is how different organizations collaborating together can bring about positive change in a neighborhood or local community. It seems unlikely that a single church or single community organization could ever have the same impact.

For Alastair, this was most striking in the Hodge Hill case study in Chapter 6, where a coalition of three grassroots organizations—one of which has grown out of the local church—are working together to support neighbors in building community in the Firs and Bromford neighborhoods and more widely across the parish. Their title for this joint work, "Together We Can," encapsulates this collaboration.

Other coalitions in the case studies in Chapter 2 are evident from those participating in the Reconciling Mission program. For example, a local community organization, Burntwood Be A Friend, is key to effecting change in the parish of St Anne's, Chasetown. While the church was the original initiator, the Burntwood Be A Friend organization has drawn in many others from the local community without a church connection. This has made it easier for the organization to work collaboratively with the local authority and other community organizations to take forward a diverse range of projects which are helping their neighborhood to flourish in imaginative ways. This approach has been reinforced through the more recent collaboration with the youth work organization, FunClub, who took the initiative in approaching the parish church.

For David, the most significant personal experience of coalition-building came in Casa Granda, Arizona. As we saw in Chapter 3, a nonprofit organization, Seeds of Hope, partnered with a local school, supportive police officers, and a brave housing manager to transform a drug-infested rental housing complex to a safer neighborhood offering affordable home ownership. Coalition-building continues to be a priority in the Casa Grande community as demonstrated by the emergence of the Faith Alliance coalition of religious and civic organizations.

While coalitions of organizations are vital to effecting change, we are mindful of the reality that "organizations cannot collaborate—only the people within them do."[12] Organizational relationships are therefore founded on the relationships among significant players within them. Organizations don't have relationships; only individual human beings do. There will therefore be a point of vulnerability when key personnel move on or retire. New relationships will need to be built with those who follow. If a successor does not share the same convictions and commitments as their predecessor, this can threaten organizational relationships and collaboration. How successors are chosen, and how batons are handed on, become important at such times of transition.

Multiplying Facilitative Leadership

Another strong thread running through the case studies is the significance of leadership. There is a dual aspect to this. Each of the case studies revealed key leaders with a deep heart for their locality and for the people of their neighborhood. The type of leadership exercised by these leaders is notable. It is characterized not by heroic leadership from the front, but more by "guiding, nurturing, supporting, and encouraging," as one of the Hodge Hill team described it. A further defining aspect of their leadership is a facilitative approach which has empowered and released others to step up and exercise leadership of their own.

This multiplication of leadership gifts and approaches has been a significant source of the power of these case studies. It may appear in what can seem like small ways. For example, Mary Sapsford, one of the co-founders of Crafty Café in Berkswich Parish, encourages local people beyond the church to share their crafting skills with others through the café.

Sometimes it may be through encouraging someone to take on a part-time paid role. In Hodge Hill, a resident called Clare was encouraged by family members and existing staff to apply to become a Street Connector trainee. She reported that, "I hadn't had a paid job for years, and really battled with myself—and my mental health—thinking about applying for this."[13] She struggled to see herself holding down a job. Becoming a paid member of a team, and having others believe in her, has grown her self-confidence and strengthened Clare's leadership within her community.

This experience reflects the adage that the essence of community development is leadership development. The ability of congregations and other community-based organizations to recruit, nurture, and support leaders that reflect the diversity of the community is a vital task. According to the Christian Community Development Association (CCDA), "The core of leadership development is identifying, mentoring, retaining, and getting out of the way of leaders already in our communities."[14]

Addressing Systemic Issues

A recurring tension that emerged throughout this book's case studies lies between attending to individuals' needs and addressing the systemic issues at the root cause of the problems being faced. The theoretical framework explored in Chapter 1, inspired by peacebuilder Adam Curle's work, highlights the importance of going beyond addressing felt needs in bringing about a society characterized by both justice and peace.

According to Tim Soerens, "Getting clear about the particularity of our parish is important if we hope to avoid the seesaw effect of prioritizing only individuals to the neglect of systems."[15] Yet, as those involved in the long-term community-building work in Hodge Hill have found, fully grasping the particularity of one's area is not enough. One of their team noted, "Community-building takes so much time, energy and care. … How do we have the time and energy to deal with the bigger stuff?"

Part of the answer to this question is likely to involve expanding the team. This could mean finding ways to draw in those who have a passion for addressing systemic issues of inequality. It could also mean identifying those who know how to help organize collective action on issues identified as a priority by people in a local neighborhood. The theoretical framework highlights that addressing systemic issues involves a journey of raising awareness of injustice and then developing strategies to challenge the systems that perpetuate them.

MICAH, the coalition of inter-religious congregations and organizations in Milwaukee described in Chapter 4, prioritizes raising awareness of injustice and challenging systems to change. MICAH has successfully executed campaigns focused on public health concerning lead abatement, criminal justice reform around mass incarceration, and confronting racism and sectarianism in the shape of white Christian nationalism. MICAH's success in addressing these issues is grounded in the fact that the leaders live in communities directly affected by these issues, combined with a proven ability to mobilize public support.

Addressing systemic issues is demanding and can be dispiriting. Raising awareness of injustice and mobilizing individuals and groups to pursue systemic change requires years of work and may well take decades to see results. Systems such as criminal justice are generally firmly established, well-funded, and resistant to change. That's why "building a team"—or a coalition—is generally required. Sustained collective action, often supported by those with experience in community organizing, is usually required for successful system change.

Depending Patiently on God

One common strand running through all this book's case studies is that they emerge from what theologian Sam Wells identifies as communities of hope.[16] These are local churches comprised of Christian disciples who recognize that they are invited to partner with God in realizing more of God's reign here on earth. In this partnership the church understands that it is not all down to her, because the fundamental work has already been accomplished by God in Jesus. The church can be a community of hope because she looks not to herself to address all the challenges of her community, but instead "together looks to the action and revelation of God."[17] Having such a dependence on God does not provide an excuse for passivity. Rather it enables the church to shoulder her share of the task, trusting that the final fulfillment of her hopes—and those of the whole world—are in God's loving, tender hands, and ultimately rest on God's tireless shoulders.

One significant aspect of this is how we think about time. "When we think in terms of decades rather than years, it changes our posture of what can happen." Tim Soerens continues, "If the game is joining God in the holistic restoration and renewal of a place, we shouldn't set our hearts on this happening in a few years. It's going to take a while. It's also going to be difficult ... "[18] Local churches need to understand that they are in this "game" for the long haul. The parish of Hodge Hill has grasped this, and their local organizations have been helped with a long-term perspective through having grant funding for their community-building spread over more than a 10-year period. While such grant funding is a rare thing, the long-term perspective at Hodge Hill is available to every congregation.

It is therefore important to remind ourselves that genuine community development and transformational justice take decades, not months or years. Of the US case studies, CLDI in Billings was founded in 1981, MICAH in Milwaukee in 1988, and Seeds of Hope in Casa Grande in 1992. In the decades since its founding, each organization has experienced setbacks—or detours, as seen in the foundational stories described in Chapter 1—leadership transitions, and the launching and ending of multiple programs. What has remained constant is a commitment to a particular place and a faith-inspired vision of a beloved community. Such a commitment requires generational work. This should come as no surprise when we look back to the foundational story of Moses's journey with Israel.

Both of our foundational Biblical narratives remind us that various types of "detour" are to be expected as part of such journeys for God's people. Perhaps more significantly, these stories also remind us that God can reintegrate such detours and transfigure them for God's good purposes. Several case studies in this book offer testimony to this truth.

When it comes to thinking in terms of generational work, part of the key is grasping the essence of the church's vocation or calling.[19] Early in the Biblical canon, God makes three promises to the chosen Abrahamic family: to make of them a great nation, to bless them, and to make their name great. The big question is *why*. God gives the clear and startling answer: "*So that* you will be a blessing." (Gen 12:2) This is the great purpose statement. This was why God chose a particular people, Israel. God goes further: so that, "in you all the families of the earth shall be blessed." It's about everyone. Now is the time for the church to realize that the mantle has been passed to her. As local churches and congregations, we are called to be a blessing to all the peoples of the earth.[20] We might ask, "How much do our neighbors recognize this about us?"

In a culture that seeks quick fixes and is prone to short-term solutions, this longer-term perspective requires the church to practice the virtue of patience. Alan Kreider highlights how central patience was as a virtue to the early Christians, who "believed that God is patient and that Jesus visibly embodied patience."[21] Such patience was manifest in the early Christians' behavior and was shaped by their formation and teaching in preparation for baptism. In a recent reflection provocatively titled *When Church Stops Working*, the authors highlight how today's church needs to embrace the invitation to wait patiently upon God, to avoid the contemporary drive to "acceleration," and to seek "resonance" with God's actions in the world.[22]

This all prompts a reminder that our current worship practices and discipleship formation will need to nurture patience and the capacity for watchful waiting, to be faithful to the image of God offered by the Biblical witness, and to take proper inspiration from the early church. Christians can be patient and wait because we are confident that God is at work by the Holy Spirit and, in collaboration with the church, will bring about a promised future that fulfills all our human longings. When we then experience a foretaste of the heavenly banquet here on earth, and have glimpsed more of that future now, we can be encouraged to be patient as we await the promised final fulfillment.[23]

Phyllis Tickle reminds us that the Christian church has experienced radical change about every 500 years since its founding. In each of these wrenching transitions, "a new, more vital form of Christianity does indeed emerge."[24] Since the last major transformation came in the 16th-century Reformation, Tickle suggests that we are due another significant shift in the 21st century. While Tickle offers various possibilities for how the latest shift might play out, we believe that local churches' faithful re-engagement with place will be one feature of this "emergence." It also means that we live in uncertain times, a liminal season of intriguing possibilities. We should therefore not be surprised if the church is unsettled and is struggling to navigate this season.[25]

The writer to the early church in Colossae was convinced that in Jesus all the fullness of God was pleased to dwell; and that, through Jesus, God was pleased to reconcile all things to God's self, "by making peace through the blood of his cross." (Col. 1:19–20) This encapsulates God's mission of bringing about a reconciliation of "all things," both on earth and in heaven. We are invited to participate in this reconciling mission of God. There is no more hopeful way to do so than through our local churches' patient engagement with our neighbors and neighborhood organizations. That is the testimony of the case studies in this book. In reading them, our hope is that you and your neighbors will be encouraged to play your part in this great adventure.

Questions for Reflection and Group Discussion

1. As you have read this book, which of these threads has been most striking for you, and why would you want to emphasize or name it?
2. Which of these threads presents the biggest challenge to your local church(es) to fully integrate into your corporate life, and why is that so? What do you want to do about this?
3. Is there an additional thread which you consider important to a local church's missional engagement with her locality which has not been named here? If there is, what is it and why do you think it matters?

Notes

Introduction

1. Albeit Roman Catholic participation rates stabilized between 2014 and 2021, after dropping between 2007 and 2014, https://www.pewresearch.org/religion/2021/12/14/about-three-in-ten-u-s-adults-are-now-religiously-unaffiliated/ (January 27, 2025)
2. Daniel A. Cox, "Generation Z and the Future of Faith in America" (Survey Center on American Life of the American Enterprise Institute: March 24, 2022), https://www.americansurveycenter.org/research/generation-z-future-of-faith/ (January 27, 2025)
3. The birth years for generations vary significantly, but for our purposes the Silent Generation was born between 1928 and 1945, Baby Boomers from 1946 to 1964, Generation X from 1965 to 1980, Millennials from 1981 to 1997, and Gen Z from 1997 to 2012. See Cox, "Generation Z and the Future of Faith in America"
4. See, for example: https://missionalmarketing.com/50-best-church-growth-books/ (January 27, 2025)
5. See, among others, Lesslie Newbigin, *The Open Secret: An Introduction to the Theology of Mission* (London: SPCK, 1995)
6. Darrell L. Guder, ed., *Missional Church: A Vision for the Sending of the Church in North America* (Grand Rapids, MI: Eerdmans Publishing, 1998)
7. See: https://www.thearda.com/us-religion/history/timelines/entry?etype=3&eid=24 (January 28, 2025)
8. Graham Cray, ed., *Mission-shaped Church: Church Planting and Fresh Expressions of Church in a Changing Context* (London: Church House Publishing, 2004); and see https://freshexpressions.org.uk/ (April 5, 2025)
9. See: https://www.pewresearch.org/science/wp-content/uploads/sites/16/2021/05/PS_2021.05.26_climate-and-generations_REPORT.pdf (January 27, 2025)
10. See, for example: https://info.uwe.ac.uk/news/uwenews/news.aspx?id=4156 (January 27, 2025)
11. See, for example, the English free church writer, Martin Robinson, *The Place of the Parish: Imagining Mission in Our Neighbourhood* (London: SCM Press, 2020)

12 For a wider consideration of current tensions around parish and new expressions of church in an English context, see Will Foulger, *Present in Every Place? The Church of England's New Churches, and the Future of the Parish* (London: SCM Press, 2023)

13 See: https://www.thebowencenter.org/bowen-theory-1 (February 2, 2025); and Israel Galindo, *The Hidden Lives of Congregations: Discerning Church Dynamics* (Herndon, VA: The Alban Institute, 2004)

14 David R. Brubaker, *Promise and Peril: Understanding and Managing Change and Conflict in Congregations* (Herndon, VA: The Alban Institute, 2009)

15 See: https://www.oxfordreference.com/display/10.1093/acref/9780191826719.001.0001/q-oro-ed4-00010671 (February 2, 2025)

16 See: https://www.bbministries.org.uk/about-us/our-history/ (January 27, 2025)

17 Some of this is summarized in Alastair McKay, *Bridgebuilding: Making Peace with Conflict in the Church* (Norwich: Canterbury Press, 2019)

18 Alastair J. M. McKay, "Practising Oversight, Friendship and Reconciliation in Church Staff Teams: A Case Study of How the Staff Teams of Two Large Anglican Churches Dealt with Disagreement in Team Meetings" (D. Min. dissertation, University of Wales, 2013) available at https://www.alastairmckay.com/writing (January 27, 2025)

19 See: https://reconciliation-initiatives.org/reconciling-mission/ (January 27, 2025)

20 Willie James Jennings, *The Christian Imagination: Theology and the Origins of Race* (New Haven, CT: Yale University Press, 2011), 9–10

21 Graham Cray, *On Mission with Jesus: Changing the Default Setting of the Church* (Norwich: Canterbury Press, 2024), 123

22 See: https://sustainingcommunity.wordpress.com/2013/08/15/what-is-abcd/ (January 27, 2025)

23 See: https://en.wikipedia.org/wiki/Congregation-based_Community_Organizing (January 27, 2025)

24 As noted above, we recognize that "parish" is usually a term peculiar to older traditions, such as Roman Catholic, Orthodox, and Anglican. However, it is increasingly also used by writers of other traditions

25 See, for example: Samuel Wells and Marcia Owen, *Living without Enemies: Being Present in the Midst of Violence* (Downers Grove, IL: IVP, 2011)

26 Explored in Pope Francis, *Evangelii Gaudium* (Apostolic Exhortation to the Bishops, Clergy, Consecrated Persons and the Lay Faithful on the Proclamation of the Gospel in Today's World) (Vatican: the Holy See, November 2013) available at: https://www.vatican.va/content/francesco/en/apost_exhortations/documents/papa-francesco_esortazione-ap_20131124_evangelii-gaudium.html (April 5, 2025)

27 See, for example: Andrew Root and Blair D. Bertrand, *When Church Stops Working: A Future for Your Congregation beyond More Money, Programs, and Innovation* (Grand Rapids, MI: Brazos Press, 2023)

Chapter 1

1. Experience presenting these models to diverse church leaders shows that a visual cue is valuable for many. The drawings are by artist Susan McKay
2. Alastair McKay, *Bridgebuilding: Making Peace with Conflict in the Church* (Norwich: Canterbury Press, 2019), 48–55
3. Adam Curle, *Making Peace* (London: Tavistock, 1971)
4. John Paul Lederach, *Building Peace: Sustainable Reconciliation in Divided Societies* (Washington, DC: USIP, 1997)
5. See the statistics from the Trussell Trust, the principal network of UK food banks: https://www.trusselltrust.org/news-and-blog/latest-stats/mid-year-stats/ (January 10, 2025)
6. Andrew Rumsey, *Parish: An Anglican Theology of Place* (Norwich: SCM Press, 2017), 128–131
7. Samuel Wells, *A Future That's Bigger Than the Past: Towards the Renewal of the Church* (Norwich: Canterbury Press, 2019), 102–107
8. Wells, *A Future That's Bigger Than the Past*, 103
9. Ann Morisy, *Journeying Out: A New Approach to Christian Mission* (London: Continuum, 2004)
10. Paulo Freire, *Pedagogy of the Oppressed* (New York: Continuum, 1997)
11. https://theclewerinitiative.org/who-we-are/about-the-clewer-initiative (January 10, 2025)
12. As reported to me by Martin Anderson, the vicar of St Mary's Norton, in the Diocese of Durham, Church of England
13. The camp continues to cast a shadow with an ongoing legacy of many migrants living rough in the Calais area: https://www.theguardian.com/world/2021/nov/02/life-death-and-limbo-in-the-calais-jungle-five-years-after-its-demolition (January 10, 2025)
14. https://reconciliation-initiatives.org/racial-justice/ (January 10, 2025)
15. For one exploration of this, see: Tim Judson, *Dark Weeping and Light Sleeping: Whiteness as a Doctrine of De-Formation* (Oxford: Regent's Park College, 2024)
16. Dr. Murray Bowen, an American psychiatrist, developed an influential theory of human relations known as (Bowen) Family Systems Theory. He identified *homeostasis*, the self-regulating process by which biological systems tend to maintain stability, as a key feature also of emotional or relational systems. See: https://bowentheoryacademy.org/bowen-theory/a-view-of-bowen-theory-from-the-21st-century (February 1, 2025)
17. https://christianclimateaction.org/who-we-are/ (January 10, 2025)
18. For an introductory articulation of the link to Christian mission, see: Grace Thomas and Mark Coleman, *Climate Action as Mission: How to Link the Gospel with Safeguarding Creation* (Cambridge: Grove Books, 2021)

19 https://ecochurch.arocha.org.uk/how-eco-church-works/ (January 10, 2025)
20 As reported to me by Philip Brent, vicar of St Lawrence's Frodingham and All Saints' New Brumby, in the Diocese of Lincoln, Church of England
21 https://www.theguardian.com/global-development/2023/nov/16/who-declares-loneliness-a-global-public-health-concern (January 10, 2025)
22 https://www.thersa.org/comment/2021/05/the-talking-revolution (January 10, 2025)
23 As reported to me by Scott Watts, who was then a team vicar of the benefice of Vale and Cotswold Edge, in the Diocese of Gloucester, Church of England
24 Marianne Rozario with Esther Platt, *Creating a Neighbourhood Health Service: The Role of Churches and Faith Groups in Social Prescribing* (London: Theos, 2025) available at https://www.theosthinktank.co.uk/cmsfiles/Report—Creating-a-Neigbourhood-Health-Service.pdf (April 5, 2025)
25 https://stmaryscpr.squarespace.com/our-story (January 10, 2025)
26 https://m.luton.gov.uk/Page/Show/Community_and_living/Luton%20observatory%20census%20statistics%20and%20mapping/population/Pages/2021-Census-ethnicity-language-nationality-and-religion.aspx (January 10, 2025)
27 Or Stephen Yaxley-Lennon, who has gone by various pseudonyms: https://en.wikipedia.org/wiki/Tommy_Robinson_(activist) (January 10, 2025). He rose to prominence again in 2024, at the time of race-related riots across the UK, garnering attention and encouragement from North American power brokers
28 Beyond Today, "How Can a Town Beat the Extremists," BBC Radio 4 (March 8, 2019) https://www.bbc.co.uk/sounds/play/p07300qb (January 10, 2025)
29 The relationships were recently seriously strained and tested as a result of the open war in Gaza and beyond, in the Middle East, after the events of October 7, 2023
30 Graham Cray, *On Mission with Jesus: Changing the Default Setting of the Church* (Norwich: Canterbury Press, 2024), 123
31 Samuel Wells, *Act Justly: Practices to Reshape the World* (Norwich: Canterbury Press, 2022), 18
32 Set out in full in, Samuel Wells, *A Nazareth Manifesto: Being with God* (Chichester: John Wiley & Sons, 2015); summarized in, Samuel Wells, *Incarnational Mission: Being with the World* (Norwich: Canterbury Press, 2018), 14–15
33 See my report of first hearing the presentation of Curle's model by John Paul Lederach: McKay, *Bridgebuilding*, 48–51
34 Other than the two midwives, none of the women in this story are named in the text
35 Likely in Arabia, east of the Gulf of Aqaba: https://en.wikipedia.org/wiki/Midian (January 10, 2025)
36 Sutherland is where the McKay/MacKay clan originally hails from, in the northern tip of Scotland: it is remote and sparsely populated
37 Wells's calculation of 90 percent seems over-generous and may ignore the time Jesus spent as a displaced person in Bethlehem and then as a refugee in Egypt, if we accept Matthew's account: see Wells, *Incarnational Mission*, 13

38 Revealed among others in, Kenneth E. Bailey, *Jesus Through Middle Eastern Eyes: Cultural Studies in the Gospels* (London: SPCK, 2008)

39 For one reading of this see: Ched Myers, *Binding the Strong Man: A Political Reading of Mark's Gospel* (Maryknoll, NY: Orbis, 1988). This section focusses primarily on Mark's gospel. The parallels are there in Matthew and Luke; and can also be discerned in John

40 Unusually, this inauguration is recorded by all four gospel writers, underlining its significance

41 John records Jesus as remaining locally for a couple of days after his baptism and then going to Galilee. (Jn 1:35–43)

42 Brought into even sharper relief by Matthew (Mt 12:46–49) and Luke (Lk 8:19–21)

43 Luke records that "the curtain of the temple was torn in two." (Lk 23:45) Matthew records that at Jesus's death, "the curtain of the temple was torn in two, from top to bottom. The earth shook, and the rocks were split. The tombs also were opened, and many bodies of the saints who had fallen asleep were raised." (Mt 27:51–52) The tearing of the temple curtain signifies the removal of the barrier separating God from the people

44 Mark and Luke prefer "kingdom of God"; Matthew prefers "kingdom of heaven". I take the two to be indistinguishable

45 While Mark does not make this so explicit, the other gospels are at pains to emphasize this. See for example: Lk 24:39–43, Mt 28:9, and Jn 20:27

46 Howard Thurman, *Jesus and the Disinherited* (Boston, MA: Beacon Press, 1996)

47 Morisy, *Journeying Out*

Chapter 2

1 See Chapter 6 for an explanation of "bumping spaces"

2 This opening story is drawn from an interview with Graham Adamson, Vicki Adamson, and Mary Sapsford on August 16, 2023

3 See: https://reconciliation-initiatives.org/reconciling-mission/ (January 27, 2025)

4 "Dwelling in the Word" is a type of group *Lectio Divina* practice which forms one of the disciplines of the Partnership for Missional Church cultural change process offered in the UK through the Church Mission Society. See: https://churchmissionsociety.org/get-involved/churches/partnership-for-missional-church/ (April 5, 2025)

5 For one recent articulation see: Cormac Russell and John McKnight, *The Connected Community: Discovering the Health, Wealth, and Power of Neighborhoods* (Oakland, CA: Berrett-Koehler, 2022). McKnight, who died in late 2024, was a pioneer of the ABCD movement

6 Al Barrett and Ruth Harley, *Being Interrupted: Reimagining the Church's Mission from the Outside In* (London: SCM Press, 2020)

7. All the facilitators have been trained in an action learning set process using an approach developed by 3D Coaching: https://www.3dcoaching.com/action-learning-set-facilitator-training/ (April 5, 2025)
8. Coventry Cathedral has a longstanding commitment to the ministry of reconciliation, and hosts a network called the Community of the Cross of Nails, of which Reconciliation Initiatives is a member. See: https://www.coventrycathedral.org.uk/reconciliation/community-of-the-cross-of-nails (April 5, 2025)
9. See: https://reconciliation-initiatives.org/reconciling-mission/ (January 27, 2025)
10. This movement is articulated in, Ann Morisy, *Journeying Out: A New Approach to Christian Mission* (London: Continuum, 2004)
11. The second and third movements are articulated in, Barrett and Harley, *Being Interrupted* (2020)
12. The three interviews were: 1) with Graham Adamson, Vicki Adamson and Mary Sapsford on August 16, 2023 in the parish of Berkswich, near Stafford, England, in the Diocese of Lichfield; 2) with Richard Westwood and Esther Allen on August 1, 2023 in the parish of St Ann's Chasetown, Burntwood, England, in the Diocese of Lichfield; and 3) with Luci Morriss and Ange Grunsell on August 8, 2023 in the Borderlink Benefice, England, in the Diocese of Hereford
13. The name of the member of the Scout association has been changed
14. Dr Joanna Sadgrove, "Reconciling Mission 2021: An Independent Evaluation—Executive Summary", March 2023, available at: https://reconciliation-initiatives.org/reconciling-mission/ (January 28, 2025)
15. For one account of an extended engagement with community-organizing within the Church of England see: Angus Ritchie, "Faith-Filled Organizing: A Decade of Change" *Crucible: The Journal of Christian Social Ethics*, The Common Good, January 2025, available at https://crucible.hymnsam.co.uk/issues/ (January 28, 2025)
16. Sadgrove, "Reconciling Mission 2021: An Independent Evaluation", 7

Chapter 3

1. Seeds of Hope homepage, www.seedsofhopeaz.com/ (January 24, 2025)
2. Christian Community Development Association homepage, www.ccda.org (January 24, 2025)
3. Jennifer Molinsky, "Housing and Livable Neighborhoods," *Joint Center for Housing Studies of Harvard University* 2021, www.jchs.harvard.edu/blog/housing-and-livable-neighborhoods(January 24, 2025)
4. Volunteer Pinal I-HELP Casa Grande Page, www.volunteerpinal.org/agency/detail/?agency_id=151938 (January 24, 2025)
5. Arnold J. Toynbee, *A Study of History, Volume III* (New York: Oxford University Press, 1934), 223

6. Mack McCarter, *How to Remake the World Neighborhood by Neighborhood* (Maryknoll, New York: Orbis Books, 2022), 40
7. McCarter, *How to Remake the World Neighborhood by Neighborhood*, 60
8. Bill Heinle, "History of FPC: The First 120 Years," *My Church Website 2016*, https://s3.amazonaws.com/mychurchwebsite/c1095/history_of_fpc.pdf (January 24, 2025)
9. Heinle, "History of FPC," 31
10. Robert Putnam developed the distinction between "bonding" and "bridging" capital is his classic *Bowling Alone: The Collapse and Revival of American Community* (New York: Simon and Schuster, 2000). For more on this see: www.socialcapitalresearch.com/difference-bonding-bridging-social-capital/ (January 29, 2025)
11. Dennis Jacobson, *Doing Justice: Congregations and Community Organizing* (Minneapolis: Fortress Press, 2017), 57

Chapter 4

1. https://worldpopulationreview.com/us-cities/wisconsin/milwaukee (January 28, 2025)
2. Barbara J. Miner, "A Look at Milwaukee's 'Shadows of Industrialization,'" *Milwaukee Magazine*, May 12, 2023, https://www.milwaukeemag.com/look-at-milwaukee-through-its-former-factories-and-the-people-who-worked-there/ (January 28, 2025)
3. *MICAH: What We Do*, https://micahmke.org/about/ (January 28, 2025)
4. WISDOM home page, https://wisdomwisconsin.org/ (January 28, 2025)
5. Gamaliel home page, https://gamaliel.org/ (January 28, 2025)
6. *MICAH: We All Belong*, https://micahmke.org/we-all-belong/ (January 28, 2025)
7. *Wikipedia: Joseph Ellwanger*, https://en.wikipedia.org/wiki/Joseph_Ellwanger (January 28, 2025)
8. Matt Pearce, "When Martin Luther King Jr. took his fight into the North, and saw a new level of hatred," *Los Angeles Times*, January 18, 2016, https://www.latimes.com/nation/la-na-mlk-chicago-20160118-story.html (January 28, 2025)
9. Coalition on Lead Emergency Home Page, https://coalitiononleademergency.org/ (January 28, 2025)
10. Alan J. Roxburgh and Fred Romanuk, *The Missional Leader: Equipping Your Church to Reach a Changing World* (San Francisco: Jossey-Bass, 2006), 5
11. Roxburgh and Romanuk, *The Missional Leader*, 60
12. F. Douglas Powe Jr. and Lovett H. Weems Jr., *Sustaining While Disrupting: The Challenge of Congregational Innovation* (Minneapolis: Fortress Press, 2022), 28
13. Terry Coy, *Return to the Margins: Understanding and Adapting as a Church to Post-Christian America* (Abbotsford, WI: Aneko Press, 2014), xxi

Chapter 5

1. "Billings, Montana," *WIKIPEDIA*, www.wikipedia.org/wiki/Billings,_Montana (January 30, 2025)
2. "About Billings," *Billings Chamber of Commerce*, www.billingschamber.com/relocate-to-billings/billings/ (January 30, 2025)
3. "South Side Neighborhood in Billings, Montana," *City-Data.com*, www.city-data.com/neighborhood/South-Side-Billings-MT.html (January 30, 2025)
4. Quote by Todd Preston in "The 40-Year Story of CLDI," *CLDI Billings*, www.youtube.com/watch?v=P05QpqaVQWs (January 30, 2025)
5. Quote by Todd Preston in "The 40-Year Story of CLDI"
6. Quote by Scott Lynch in "The 40-Year Story of CLDI"
7. Home Page of CLDI website, www.cldibillings.org/ (January 30, 2025)
8. Home Page of Rail//Line Coffee website, www.raillinecoffee.com (January 30, 2025)
9. Quote from the Home page of CLDI website, www.cldibillings.org/
10. Quote from the Programs page of CLDI website, www.cldibillings.org/programs/ (January 30, 2025)
11. Quote from the Rail//Line page of CLDI website, www.cldibillings.org/rail-line/
12. Quote by Eric Basye in "The 40-Year Story of CLDI"
13. Home Page of Dream Center, Los Angeles, www.dreamcenter.org/ (January 30, 2025)
14. Robert B. Lupton, *Return Flight* (Atlanta, GA: FCS Urban Ministries, 1997)
15. "How Churches Really Spend Their Money," *Tithely* 2019, https://get.tithe.ly/blog/how-churches-really-spend-their-money-20-fascinating-data-points-a-new-study (January 30, 2025)
16. Mark Thiessen Nation, *Discipleship in a World Full of Nazis: Recovering the True Legacy of Dietrich Bonhoeffer* (Eugene, OR: Cascade Books, 2022), 46
17. Elise Gould, "Inequality is the Main Cause of Persistent Poverty," *Economic Policy Institute 2014*, www.epi.org/blog/inequality-main-persistent-poverty/ (January 30, 2025)
18. Rebecca Haffajee and Michelle M. Mello, "Drug Companies Liability for the Opioid Epidemic," *PubMed Central* 2017, https://pmc.ncbi.nlm.nih.gov/articles/PMC7479783/ (January 30, 2025)
19. "Wall Street has spent billions buying homes. A crackdown is looming," *Fox Business*, April 29, 2024, www.foxbusiness.com/markets/wall-street-spent-billions-buying-homes-a-crackdown-is-looming (January 30, 2025)
20. "CCDA's Beginnings," Christian Community Development Association website, www.ccda.org/ccdas-beginnings/ (January 30, 2025)
21. "CCDA Justice Initiatives," www.ccda.org/justice-initiatives/ (January 30, 2025)
22. Dave R. Hagstrom, *A Mandate for Good Works: The Power of Love and Resource Management* (Billings, MT: Community Leadership and Development Inc., 1989), 37
23. Tim Soerens, *Everywhere You Look: Discovering the Church Right Where You Are* (Downers Grove, IL: IVP, 2020), 121

Chapter 6

1. This story is taken from: Al Barrett & Ruth Harley, *Being Interrupted: Re-imagining the Church's Mission from the Outside, In* (London: SCM Press, 2020), 141
2. https://resources.depaul.edu/abcd-institute/publications/publications-by-topic/Documents/ABCD-%20The%20Essentials%20-2.pdf (December 31, 2024)
3. John Kretzmann & John McKnight, *Building Communities from the Inside Out: A Path Toward Finding and Mobilizing a Community's Assets* (Chicago, IL: ACTA Publications, 1993)
4. Cormac Russell & John McKnight, *The Connected Community: Discovering the Health, Wealth and Power of Neighborhoods* (Oakland, CA: Berrett-Koehler, 2022)
5. This and subsequent quotations are taken from three interviews: with Al Barrett on August 3, 2023; and separately with Paul Wright and Penny Hall on August 3, 2023, both in Hodge Hill Parish; and with Jane Perry on November 3, 2023, via the Zoom platform
6. In the UK, where this chapter is set, an "estate" generally comprises low-income housing owned by the local authority and sometimes also by private landlords. In contrast, in the US, an "estate" typically comprises up-market privately-owned mansion housing. North American readers will therefore need to make a suitable mental adjustment
7. This included drawing on a process resource developed by the Church Urban Fund entitled *Know Your Church, Know Your Neighbourhood*, see https://cuf.org.uk/know-your-church-know-your-neighbourhood (January 27, 2025)
8. Timebanking UK is the national charity supporting the development of timebanking across the country, see https://timebanking.org/ (April 6, 2025)
9. An initiative of the Church Urban Fund, see https://cuf.org.uk/places-of-welcome (January 27, 2025)
10. Bingo is a game in which players mark off numbers on distributed cards as the numbers are drawn randomly by a caller. The winner being the first person to mark off all their numbers
11. See https://www.yourlocalpantry.co.uk/ (January 27, 2025)
12. Ann Morisy, *Beyond the Good Samaritan: Community Ministry and Mission* (London: Continuum, 2009)
13. This idea is developed more fully by Andrew Grinnell, "Beyond 'Assets and Deficits' to 'Gifts and Wounds'", *Crucible: The Journal of Christian Social Ethics*, The Politics and Theology of Place, October 2019, available at https://crucible.hymnsam.co.uk/articles/2019/october/articles/beyond-assets-and-deficits-to-gifts-and-wounds/ (December 16, 2024)
14. For one theologically-grounded articulation of the community organizing approach in a British context see: Angus Ritchie, *Inclusive Populism: Creating Citizens in the Global Age* (Notre Dame, IN: University of Notre Dame Press, 2019)

15 Matthew 14:13–21, Mark 6:30–44, Luke 9:10–17, and John 6:1–15
16 As an example of a limitation, it is unclear how everyone's gifts and neighborliness are drawn upon, although given the large numbers of people involved it seems hard to believe that there was not a huge cooperative effort, rather than a reliance on just the 12 core disciples

Chapter 7

1 For a North American example, see Paul Sparks, Tim Soerens, and Dwight J. Friesen, *The New Parish: How Neighborhood Churches Are Transforming Mission, Discipleship and Community* (Downers Grove, IL: IVP, 2014); for an English example, see Martin Robinson, *The Place of the Parish: Imagining Mission in Our Neighbourhood* (London: SCM Press, 2020)
2 John L. McKnight: "Defining 'community' and 'neighborhood'," https://youtu.be/3UpOSFL5mq4 (January 1, 2025)
3 Sparks, Soerens, and Friesen, *The New Parish*, 23
4 Tim Soerens, *Everywhere You Look: Discovering the Church Right Where You Are* (Downers Grove, IL: IVP, 2020), 68
5 Soerens, *Everywhere You Look*, 70
6 Nancy Tatom Ammerman, *Congregation and Community* (New Brunswick, NJ: Rutgers University Press, 2001), 370
7 Explored in texts such as Eugene H. Peterson, *Under the Unpredictable Plant: An Exploration in Vocational Holiness* (Grand Rapids, MI: William B. Eerdmans, 1992)
8 Soerens, *Everywhere You Look*, 101
9 For several English illustrations of this see Al Barrett, ed., *Finding the Treasure: Good News from the Estates* (London: SPCK, 2023)
10 For an insightful critique of this in relation to the Church of England, see Al Barrett, "Simpler, Humbler, Bolder?" *Crucible: The Journal of Christian Social Ethics*, Simpler, Humbler, Bolder? Smaller Church Theology, July 2024, available at https://crucible.hymnsam.co.uk/articles/2024/july/articles/simpler-humbler-bolder/ (December 31, 2024)
11 Soerens, *Everywhere You Look*, 103
12 Soerens, *Everywhere You Look*, 92
13 Together We Can 2: Progress Report, Year 2, July 2023, 17, available at https://worthunlimited.co.uk/file/worth/twc2-year-2-progress-report-v2-86591.pdf (January 16, 2025)
14 https://ccda.org/about/philosophy/leadership-development/?gad_source=1 (January 15, 2025)
15 Soerens, *Everywhere You Look*, 68

16 Samuel Wells, *A Future That's Bigger Than the Past: Towards the Renewal of the Church* (Norwich: Canterbury Press, 2019), 138–142
17 Wells, *A Future That's Bigger Than the Past*, 141
18 Soerens, *Everywhere You Look*, 116
19 The centrality of parish vocation is helpfully drawn out in Will Foulger, *Present in Every Place? The Church of England's New Churches, and the Future of the Parish* (London: SCM Press, 2023)
20 For one take on this, see Robin Greenwood, *Sharing God's Blessing: How to Renew the Local Church* (London: SPCK, 2016)
21 Alan Kreider, *The Patient Ferment of the Early Church: The Improbable Rise of Christianity in the Roman Empire* (Grand Rapids, MI: Baker Academic, 2016), 1
22 Andrew Root and Blair D. Bertrand, *When Church Stops Working: A Future for Your Congregation beyond More Money, Programs, and Innovation* (Grand Rapids, MI: Brazos Press, 2023)
23 Pope Francis, *Evangelii Gaudium* (Apostolic Exhortation to the Bishops, Clergy, Consecrated Persons and the Lay Faithful on the Proclamation of the Gospel in Today's World) (Vatican: the Holy See, November 2013), 170–172. Available at: https://www.vatican.va/content/francesco/en/apost_exhortations/documents/papa-francesco_esortazione-ap_20131124_evangelii-gaudium.html (April 5, 2025)
24 Phyllis Tickle, *The Great Emergence: How Christianity is Changing and Why* (Grand Rapids, MI: Baker Books, 2009), 17
25 For one reflection on this, see Jeffrey Jones and David Fredrickson, *Being Church in a Liminal Time: Remembering, Letting Go, Resurrecting* (Lanham, MD: Rowman and Littlefield, 2023)

Recommended Further Reading and Resources

Selected Bibliography

Aldous, Benjamin, Harvey Kwiyani, Peniel Rajkumar, and Victoria Turner, eds. *Lived Mission in 21st Century Britain: Ecumenical and Postcolonial Perspectives*. London: SCM Press, 2024.
Ammerman, Nancy Tatom. *Congregation & Community*. New Brunswick, NJ: Rutgers University Press, 1997.
Barrett, Al, ed. *Finding the Treasure: Good News from the Estates*. London: SPCK, 2023.
Barrett, Al, and Ruth Harley. *Being Interrupted: Re-imagining the Church's Mission from the Outside, In*. London: SCM Press, 2020.
Beaumont, Susan. *How to Lead When You Don't Know Where You're Going: Leading in a Liminal Season*. Lanham, MD: Rowman and Littlefield, 2019.
Block, Peter. *Community: The Structure of Belonging*. San Francisco, CA: Berrett-Koehler Publishers, Inc., 2008.
Bridges, William. *Managing Transitions: Making the Most of Change (2nd edition)*. Cambridge, MA: Perseus Books Group, 2003.
Brown, Adrienne Maree. *Emergent Strategy: Shaping Change, Changing Worlds*. Chico, CA: AK Press, 2017.
Brubaker, David R. *Promise and Peril: Understanding and Managing Change and Conflict in Congregations*. Herndon, VA: The Alban Institute, 2009.
Cameron, Helen. *Just Mission: Practical Politics for Local Churches*. London: SCM Press, 2015.
Coy, Terry. *Return to the Margins: Understanding and Adapting as a Church to Post-Christian America*. Abbotsford, WI: Aneko Press, 2014.
Cray, Graham. *On Mission with Jesus: Changing the Default Setting of the Church*. Norwich: Canterbury Press, 2024.
Curle, Adam. *Making Peace*. London: Tavistock, 1971.
Foulger, Will. *Present in Every Place? The Church of England's New Churches, and the Future of the Parish*. London: SCM Press, 2023.

Francis, Pope. *Evangelii Gaudium* (Apostolic Exhortation to the Bishops, Clergy, Consecrated Persons and the Lay Faithful on the Proclamation of the Gospel in Today's World). Vatican: the Holy See, November 24, 2013.

Galindo, Israel. *The Hidden Lives of Congregations: Discerning Church Dynamics*. Herndon, VA: Alban Institute, 2004.

Greenwood, Robin. *Sharing God's Blessing: How to Renew the Local Church*. London: SPCK, 2016.

Guder, Darrell L., ed. *Missional Church: A Vision for the Sending of the Church in North America*. Grand Rapids, MI: Eerdmans Publishing, 1998.

Hester, Richard L., and Kelli Walker-Jones. *Know Your Story and Lead with It: The Power of Narrative in Clergy Leadershp*. Herndon, VA: The Alban Institute, 2009.

Hunter, James Davison. *To Change the World: The Irony, Tragedy, & Possibility of Christianity in the Late Modern World*. New York, NY: Oxford University Press, 2010.

Jacobsen, Dennis A. *Doing Justice: Congregations and Community Organizing (2nd edition)*. Minneapolis, MN: Fortress Press, 2017.

Jennings, Willie James. *The Christian Imagination: Theology and the Origins of Race*. New Haven, CT: Yale University Press, 2011.

Johnson, Barry. *Polarity Management: Identifying and Managing Unsolvable Problems*. Amherst, MA: HRD Press, 1992.

Kreider, Alan. *The Patient Ferment of the Early Church: The Improbable Rise of Christianity in the Roman Empire*. Grand Rapids, MI: Baker Academic, 2016.

Kresta, David E. *Jesus on Main Street: Good News Through Community Economic Development*. Eugene, OR: Cascade Books, 2021.

Kretzmann, John P., and John McKnight, *Building Communities from the Inside Out: A Path Toward Mobilizing a Community's Assets*. Skokie, IL: ACTA Publications, 1993.

Jones, Jeffrey, and David Fredrickson. *Being Church in a Liminal Time: Remembering, Letting Go, Resurrecting*. Lanham, MD: Rowman and Littlefield, 2023.

Judson, Tim. *Dark Weeping and Light Sleeping: Whiteness as a Doctrine of De-Formation*. Oxford: Regent's Park College, 2024.

Lewis, Robert, and Wayne Cordeiro. *Culture Shift: Transforming Your Church from the Inside Out*. San Francisco, CA: Jossey-Bass, 2005.

Loudon, Ellen, ed. *12 Rules for Christian Activists: A Toolkit for Massive Change*. Norwich: Canterbury Press, 2020.

McCarter, Mack, with Tim Muldoon. *How to Remake the World Neighborhood by Neighborhood*. Maryknoll, NY: Orbis Books, 2022.

McKay, Alastair. *Bridgebuilding: Making Peace with Conflict in the Church*. Norwich: Canterbury Press, 2019.

McKnight, John, and Peter Block. *The Abundant Community: Awakening the Power of Families and Neighborhoods*. Oakland, CA: Berrett-Koehler, 2012.

Morisy, Ann. *Beyond the Good Samaritan: Community Ministry and Mission.* London: Continuum, 2009.

Morisy, Ann. *Journeying Out: A New Approach to Christian Mission.* London: Continuum, 2004.

Myers, Ched. *Binding the Strong Man: A Political Reading of Mark's Gospel.* Maryknoll, NY: Orbis, 1988.

Newbigin, Lesslie. *The Open Secret: An Introduction to the Theology of Mission.* London: SPCK, 1995.

Peterson, Eugene H. *Under the Unpredictable Plant: An Exploration in Vocational Holiness.* Grand Rapids, MI: William B. Eerdmans, 1992.

Powe, F. Douglas Jr., and Lovett H. Weems Jr. *Sustaining While Disrupting: The Challenge of Congregational Innovation.* Minneapolis, MN: Fortress Press, 2022.

Rendle, Gil. *Countercultural: Subversive Resistance and the Neighborhood Congregation.* Lanham, MD: Rowman & Littlefield, 2023.

Rendle, Gil, and Alice Mann. *Holy Conversation: Strategic Planning as a Spiritual Practice for Congregations.* Herdon, VA: The Alban Institute, 2003.

Ritchie, Angus. *Inclusive Populism: Creating Citizens in the Global Age.* Notre Dame, IN: University of Notre Dame Press, 2019.

Robinson, Martin. *The Place of the Parish: Imagining Mission in Our Neighbourhood.* London: SCM Press, 2020.

Rooms, Nigel, and Patrick Keifert. *Forming a Missional Church: Creating Deep Cultural Change in Congregations.* Cambridge: Grove Books, 2014.

Rooms, Nigel. *Missional Church: What Does Good Look Like?* Cambridge: Grove Books, 2019.

Root, Andrew, and Blair D. Bertrand. *When Church Stops Working: A Future for Your Congregation beyond More Money, Programs, and Innovation.* Grand Rapids, MI: Brazos Press, 2023.

Roxburgh, Alan J., and Fred Romanuk. *The Missional Leader: Equipping Your Church to Reach a Changing World.* San Francisco, CA: Jossey-Bass, 2006.

Rumsey, Andrew. *Parish: An Anglican Theology of Place.* London: SCM Press, 2017.

Russell, Cormac, and John McKnight. *The Connected Community: Discovering the Health, Wealth and Power of Neighborhoods.* Oakland, CA: Berrett-Koehler, 2022.

Salvatierra, Alexia, and Peter Heltzel. *Faith-Rooted Organizing: Mobilizing the Church in Service to the World.* Downers Grove, IL: InterVarsity Press, 2014.

Sanders, Alvin. *Uncommon Church: Community Transformation for the Common Good.* Downers Grove, IL: InterVarsity Press, 2020.

Schuman, Andrew. *Appreciative Inquiry: Strategically Discerning a Church's Future.* Cambridge: Grove Books, 2018.

Snow, Luther K. *The Power of Asset Mapping: How Your Congregation Can Act on its Gifts.* Herndon, VA: The Alban Institute, 2004.

Soerens, Tim. *Everywhere You Look: Discovering the Church Right Where You Are*. Downers Grove, IL: IVP, 2020.

Sparks, Paul, Tim Soerens, and Dwight J. Friesen. *The New Parish: How Neighborhood Churches are Transforming Mission, Discipleship and Community*. Downers Grove, IL: InterVarsity Press, 2014.

Steinke, Peter L. *Uproar: Calm Leadership in Anxious Times*. Lanham, MD: Rowman & Littlefield, 2019.

Swanson, Eric, and Rick Rusaw. *The Externally Focused Quest: Becoming the Best Church FOR the Community*. Minneapolis, MN: Fortress Press, 2020.

Thomas, Grace, and Mark Coleman. *Climate Action as Mission: How to Link the Gospel with Safeguarding Creation*. Cambridge: Grove Books, 2021.

Thurman, Howard, *Jesus and the Disinherited*. Boston, MA: Beacon Press, 1996.

Tickle, Phyllis. *The Great Emergence: How Christianity Is Changing and Why*. Grand Rapids, MI: Baker Books, 2008.

Wells, Samuel. *A Future That's Bigger Than the Past: Catalyzing Kingdom Communities*. Norwich: Canterbury Press, 2019.

Wells, Samuel. *Act Justly: Practices to Reshape the World*. Norwich: Canterbury Press, 2022.

Wells, Samuel. *Incarnational Mission: Being with the World*. Norwich: Canterbury Press, 2018.

Wells, Samuel, and Marcia Owen. *Living without Enemies: Being Present in the Midst of Violence*. Downers Grove, IL: IVP, 2011.

Selected Relevant Organizations

ABCD Institute is the center in the USA for a movement that considers local assets as the primary building blocks of sustainable community development. The Institute grows out of the work of John McNight and his colleagues: https://resources.depaul.edu/abcd-institute/Pages/default.aspx

Alban at Duke Divinity is the successor of the Alban Institute in the USA, and offers a range of resources for congregations and their leaders, including a useful weekly newsletter with links to short articles, edited by Prince Rivers: https://alban.org/

Barna Group conducts extensive research on congregations, communities, and cultural trends in North America, and publishes periodic reports on relevant trends. One relevant example, "Inside the Urban Church: How local congregations engage with and impact their communities." Available at: https://www.barna.com/

Centre for Theology and Community is an English not-for-profit based in east London, which grew out of local churches involved in community organizing, and works with churches from a wide range of denominations and traditions and in strategic partnership with Citizens UK, led by Angus Ritchie: https://www.ctcuk.org/

Christian Community Development Association (CCDA) supports a network of more than 1,000 congregations and faith-based organizations across the US that are significantly engaged with their local communities: https://ccda.org/

Church Urban Fund (CUF) was established by the Church of England, following the 1985 *Faith in the City* report, as a practical response to unmet social need. CUF coordinates the Together Network, a union of 21 faith-based partnerships across England, driven by the desire to end poverty. CUF has published the *Growing Good* resource, a free six-session course helping churches explore the connection between social action, discipleship and growth. See: https://cuf.org.uk/organisational-streams/together-network; and, https://growing-good.org.uk/

Congregational Consulting Group (CCG) is composed primarily of former Alban Institute consultants in North America, and includes several consultants with significant experience in organizational and community development, including David Brubaker. Their "Perspectives" blog features articles from CCG consultants: https://www.congregationalconsulting.org/

HeartEdge is an international network of people and churches growing compassionate response to need, cultural and commercial activity, and congregational life: an initiative of St Martin-in-the-Fields, London, England, inspired by the theological vision of Samuel Wells: https://www.heartedge.org/

Nurture Development is the leading ABCD organization in Ireland and Britain linked to the ABCD Institute, led by Cormac Russell: https://www.nurturedevelopment.org/

Parish Collective is a North American movement "connecting people to be the church in the neighborhood." Through learning communities, resources, and events, the Parish Collective encourages practitioners to be part of the new parish movement: https://www.parishcollective.org/

Together for the Common Good is an English not-for-profit that helps people to play their part in strengthening the bonds of social trust within their neighborhoods and localities, led by Jenny Sinclair: https://togetherforthecommongood.co.uk/

Reconciliation Initiatives is an English not-for-profit providing learning and development programs for clergy and lay leaders primarily in Britain, including the *Reconciling Mission* program with a principal focus on missional engagement with local neighborhoods, led by Alastair McKay: https://reconciliation-initiatives.org/

Index

A Rocha 20
Aaron 31
Acts
    5:5–12 69–70
    19 97–8
Adams, Peter 22–3
Adamson, Graham 47–8, 51–2, 53, 63–4, 68
Adamson, Vicki 47–8, 51–2, 58–9, 68
Allen, Esther 55, 56, 63, 67
Ammerman, Nancy Tatom 139
Anderson, Jay 89
Asset-Based Community Development (ABCD)
    community ecology and death 131–2
    description 10, 114–16
    growth and territoriality 130–1
    individuals' fragilities 129–30
    mental health challenges 128–9
    Reconciling Mission 49–50
    as a spectrum 131
    structures and personality tensions 129
awareness of injustice 17–19, 83, 96, 101, 108, 134, 143, 144

Baby Boomers 2
Barrett, Al
    Asset-Based Community Development (ABCD) 50, 115
    bumping spaces 119
    church neighborhood 116, 125
    community-building 130, 132–3
    community connectors 117–18
    community ecology 131–2
    leadership 127–8
    mental health challenges 128
    organizational structure 129
    street parties 120
    timebanking 117
basic human needs 15–16
Basye, Eric 102, 108
Being White (program) 18
Berkswich parish church 65–6, 138–9
Big Local program 115–16
Billings, Montana 99–102, 104, 107–110, 139–40, 145
Bonhoeffer, Dietrich 105
Borderlink Benefice 54, 65, 66
Bowen, Murray 19
Bridge Builders 4–5
Brubaker, David 4–5, 71–2
bumping spaces 48, 119–21
Burntwood Be A Friend 56–7, 67, 141
butterfly and empowerment 103–4

Cabana Neighborhood 72–73
Casa Grande, Arizona 71–3, 75, 81–5, 91, 101, 141, 145, 153
charitable acts 15–16, 85
Christendom 97
Christian Climate Action 20
Christian Community Development Association (CCDA) 71, 75, 108, 143
Christian faith 41, 83
Church of England 5, 17, 18, 49, 54, 61, 62, 138
Clewer Initiative 17–18
Coalition On Lead Emergency (COLE) 92
coalitions 7–8
community advocacy 96
community-building 96
    framework assessment 132–4
    growth and leadership 127–8
    growth and territoriality 130–1

Hodge Hill Church 116–25
    individual and community level impact 126–7
    paid community connectors 125–6
community connectors 117–18, 120, 122, 125–6
community development 7, 71, 73–5, 100, 101, 105, 109, 110–11, 142, 145
Community Leadership and Development Inc. (CLDI)
    background 99–101
    cost of discipleship 104–5
    framework analysis 107–8
    individual motivations 101–4
    joys and challenges 105–7
    learnings 108–10
compassion 15, 77, 79, 91, 102, 126
    limits of 79–80
congregational participation, declining 1–2
congregational revitalization 2
Congregation-Based Community Organizing (CBCO) 10
conscientization 17
corporate redistribution 73
Covid-19 15, 16, 20, 47–8, 55–6, 64, 121–2, 128
Coy, Terry 97
craft activities 48–9, 68
Crafty Café 48–9, 58–9, 66, 68
crucifixion 41–3
Curle, Adam 13–14, 15–16, 24–5, 26, 43–4, 143

Demetrius 98
detour 6, 28–9, 33, 34, 36–7, 38, 44, 65, 102, 116–17, 145
Diocese of Lincoln 20–1
disruption 95–8

Eco Church 20–1
Elgin, Paul 76, 79
Ellwanger, Joe 88–9, 90, 92–3
Emerling, Jeromy 104–5
empowerment 6, 7, 10, 16, 21, 23, 67, 87, 92, 101, 103, 109, 120, 121, 123–4, 130, 142
English Defence League (EDL) 22–3

Evangelical Protestant Church 1–2
Extinction Rebellion 20

facilitative leadership 142–3
Faisal, Rehana 23
Faith Alliance 75–7, 82–3, 91, 141
faith-based 73, 75, 84, 85, 93, 94, 100, 163
Farmery, Keith 20
Feeding of 5,000 (John and Mark) 135–6
Firs & Bromford Neighbours Together 115, 117, 124
First Christian Church (Billings, MT) 104, 105
First Presbyterian Church of Casa Grande (AZ) 71, 75, 76, 79, 81, 82
Fitzgibbons, Lisa Navarro 76–7
flags, prayer 47–8
food banks 15, 67, 124
Ford, Tom 73
foundational stories
    Jesus's journey with Israel 35–43
    Moses's journey with Israel 26–34
Freire, Paulo 17
FunClub 64–5, 141

Gamaliel 87–8
gay pride festival 54, 65, 68
Geiger, John 100, 102
Generation Z 2
God
    dependence on 144–6
    dreams of 138
    integrating detours 44, 65
    kindness and gentleness 5
    kingdom of 24, 42, 125, 132, 152
    missionary nature 2
    patience 1, 137, 144–6
    questions 62–3
    reconciling 8, 24, 41, 44, 146
    reign of 9, 13, 14, 19, 24, 33, 34, 42, 138, 144
grant funding 144–5
Grunsell, Ange 54, 68

Hagstrom, Dave 109
Hall, Penny 122–3, 124
Hannah House 100–2, 105, 139
Harley, Ruth 50

Hay Pride 54
Heinle, Bill 76, 79
Herod 36–7
Hodge Hill Church
    bumping spaces 119–20
    community connectors 117–18
    development of individuals 123–4
    facilitative leadership 142–3
    getting to know the neighborhood 116
    grant funding 144–5
    local church and theological articulation 124–5
    mental health challenges 128–9
    negative energy 122–3
    neighbor-led activities 121–2, 123
    Open Door Community Foundation 115
    organizational coalitions 141
    respectful relationships 140
    street parties 120–1, 138
    timebanking 116–17
Homeless Emergency Lodging Program 75
horizontal reconciliation 73

Ingram, Earl, Jr. 87
Islam 91
Israelites 26, 27, 29–34, 38

Jackson, Joseph 89, 90, 92, 94
Jacobson, Dennis 85
Jennings, Willie James 9
Jesus's journey with Israel 35
    crucifixion and death 41–2
    driven into the wilderness 38
    flight to Egypt 36–7
    infancy of Jesus 36
    learning in Nazareth 37
    public ministry and confrontation 39–40
    resurrection 42
Jones, Lisa 89–90
Joseph 36–7
The Jungle 18

King, Martin Luther, Jr. 88, 90
Koinonia Management Company (KMC) 100

Koinonia Mexican Restaurant 100
Kreider, Alan 145
Kretzmann, Jody 114
Kroll, Tabitha 105–6

Lawson, James 88
leadership development 100–1, 109, 110, 142–3
Lederach, John Paul 13
Lemberg, Rick 76, 81–2
Lennon, Stephen 22
Lincoln, Diocese of 20–1
local congregations, importance of 3, 6–7
loneliness 21, 67
Lupton, Bob 103
Luton, UK 22–3
Lynch, Scott 100

Mark 6:7–13 110–11
Mary 36–7, 44
Matthew 25:31–46 84–5
McCarter, Mack 80–1
McEuen, Scott 75–6, 78, 79, 83
McFarland, Craig 83
McKay, Alastair 4, 5–6, 149, 150, 151
McKnight, John 114–15, 137
men's mental health 55–6, 67
Men's Wellbeing Walk 67
mental health 21, 48, 55–6, 63, 67–8, 79, 128–9, 142
Midian 29–30, 34, 37, 44
Millenials 2
Miller, Marilyn 88–9, 91–2
Milwaukee, Wisconsin 84, 87–92, 97, 101, 143, 145
Milwaukee Inner-City Congregations Allied for Hope (MICAH)
    background 87–9
    compassion and justice 91–3
    framework assessment 96–7
    individual motivations 89–91
    leadership for change 93–5
    learnings 96
    systemic issues 143–4
    time taken for community development and transformational justice 145
missional 2–3, 5, 6, 8–9, 10, 24, 50–1, 60–1, 64, 70, 93–4, 136, 147

missional church movement 2–3, 148
missional journey 13, 14, 19, 21, 24, 26, 137
Morisy, Ann 16, 125, 150, 152, 153, 156, 161
Morriss, Luci 54, 59–60, 66, 68
Moses's journey with Israel 26
   being raised in Pharaoh's house 27–8
   confronting Pharaoh 31
   crossing the Red Sea 32
   journeying towards the Promised
     Land 33
   killing an Egyptian 28–9
   Midian 29–30
movements 22, 50–1, 108–9
Muslim 23, 87, 91, 120

Nazareth 36, 37, 43, 110, 151
negative energy 122–3
neighborhoods 3, 6, 8, 50, 71–2, 87, 89, 91–2, 110, 113, 114–5, 117–8, 124, 137–9, 141
neighbor-led activities 121–2, 123
Newbigin, Lesslie 2
Nunez, Antonia 77–79
Nurture Development 115

Open Door Community Foundation 115, 116, 118, 119, 120, 121, 124
organizational coalitions 7, 81, 86, 137, 141–2
outward-facing 50, 52, 62, 70, 96
outward focus 83

paid community connectors 125–6
parish 3, 7, 10, 15, 18, 20–1, 47, 51–3, 55, 61, 63–4, 65–6, 114, 138
patience 145–6
Paul 41–2, 84, 97
Perdew, Kaleb 103, 106–7
Perkins, John 71, 108
Perry, Jane 121, 123, 125, 126, 127, 130, 131
Perry, Will 90–1
personal responsibility 73–4
Peter 42, 69–70
Pharaoh 27–8, 28–32, 34
place, identity with a 137–9
Places of Welcome 119
Powe, Douglas 94–5
Price, Doug 72

Price, Peter 6
Project YES (Youth Engaged in
   Service) 74
Promised Land 33–4
Protestant denominations 1–2

Rail//Line Coffee Shop 100, 101, 139
reconciliation 8–9, 24, 41, 43, 44, 73, 146, 149, 150, 153
Reconciliation Initiatives 6, 18
Reconciling Mission 24–5
   awareness of injustice 17–19
   background 6, 49–50
   centrality of relationship-building 65–6
   challenging the system 19–21
   church becoming a guest 51, 54–5
   cultural shift and polarity management 59–61
   definition 8
   detours 64–5
   exploring uncomfortable ground and asking deeper questions 55–8
   foundational stories 43–4
   framework assessment 66–9
   meeting basic human needs 15–16
   mutual flourishing and humbly receiving 58–9
   organizational coalitions 141
   purpose of the church 61–2
   realizing more of God's reign 24
   shifting from church to God questions 62–3
   shifting the thinking about local community 51–3
   small churches accepting having enough 63–4
   transforming systems 22–3
redistribution 73
Red Sea 32
relationship-building 23, 65–6, 73–4, 80–2, 116
relocation 71, 74–5
respectful relationships 139–40
responsibility 73–5, 123, 130, 135
resurrection 41–3
Robinson, Tommy 22
Roman Catholic Church 1, 3, 83
Romanuk, Fred 93–4

Roxburgh, Alan 93–4
Rumsey, Andrew 15
Russell, Cormac 115

Sadgrove, Joanna 50, 66, 68–9
Sapsford, Mary 49, 52, 58–9, 142
Schaider, Cindy 76, 77–8, 80
Seeds of Hope
   background 71
   framework assessment 83–4
   individual motivations for involvement in 77–9
   learnings 82–3
   limits of compassion 79–80
   organizational coalitions 141
   relationship-building 80–2
   Three Rs of Christian Community Development: Relocation, Reconciliation, and Redistribution 72–7
Shaw, Richard 89, 90, 92
Silent Generation 2
slavery 17–18, 31, 33
Smith, Jessica 101–2
Soerens, Tim 109–10, 138, 139, 143, 144
St Anne's, Chasetown 53, 55–8, 61, 63, 64–6, 67, 138–9, 141
St Martin-in-the-Fields 5
St Mary's Centre for Peace and Reconciliation 22, 23
street connectors 117–18, 120, 122, 125–6, 134, 142
street parties 113–14, 120–1, 138
strengths-based approaches 114
sustaining actions 96
systemic change 84, 96, 108, 110
systemic issues 8, 11, 108, 133–4, 136, 137, 143–4
systemic transformation 23, 41

talking revolution 21, 67
Tempe, Arizona 75
Temple, William 4
Thompson, Kaylee 103, 106

Three Rs of Christian Community Development: Relocation, Reconciliation, and Redistribution 72–7
Thunberg, Greta 20
Tickle, Phyllis 146
timebanking 116–17
Together We Can 115–16, 126–7, 134, 141
Toynbee, Arnold 80
transforming systems 22–3, 110, 111
trust 33, 60, 81–2, 109–10

Vanderheyden, Mark 75, 82
vertical reconciliation 73
Vivian, C. T. 88

Walton, Chuck 81–2
Webster, Patti 100
Wells, Sam 5, 15, 25, 144, 149, 150, 151, 158, 162, 163
Westwood, Richard 53, 56–8, 61–3, 64–5, 66, 67
Wheems, Lovett 94–5
Wilde, Oscar 15
WISDOM 87, 90
World Health Organization 21
Worth Unlimited 115, 123
Wright, Paul
   Asset-Based Community Development (ABCD) training 115
   bumping spaces 119
   church building 125
   community-building 121–2, 133–4
   community connectors 117–18
   individuals' fragilities 129
   leadership 127–8
   paid community connectors 126
   street parties 120

Young, Andrew 88
Your Local Pantry network 124
Youth for Christ (YFC) 64

Zipporah 30